THE DOMINICANS

THE DOMINICANS

By
JOHN-BAPTIST REEVES, O.P.

LONDON: SHEED & WARD

NIHIL OBSTAT :

FR. RICCARDUS KEHOE, O.P., S.T.L.

FR. QUENTINUS JOHNSON, O.P., S.T.L.

IMPRIMATUR :

FR. BEDA JARRETT, O.P.,

PRIOR PROVINCIALIS ANGLIÆ.

OCT. 27, 1929. IN FESTO D. CHRISTI REGIS.

NIHIL OBSTAT :

T. McLAUGHLIN, D.D.

CENSOR DEPUTATUS

IMPRIMATUR :

EDM : CAN : SURMONT

VIC : GEN

WESTMONASTERII, DIE VIA NOVEMBRIS

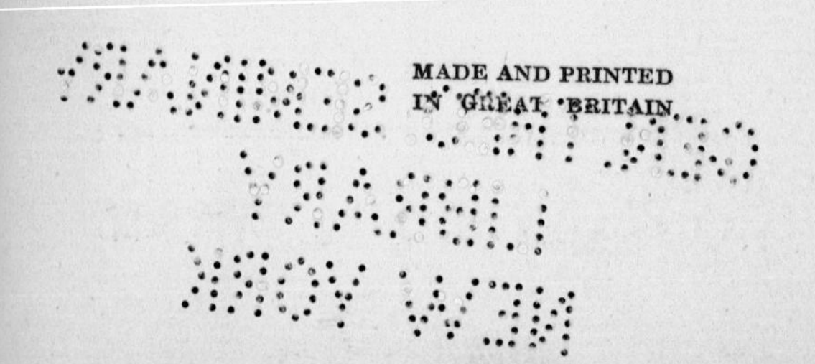

MADE AND PRINTED
IN GREAT BRITAIN

THE "MANY MANSIONS" SERIES

GENERAL EDITOR: ALGAR THOROLD.

It is intended by means of this series to bring together in an easily accessible form essays on the spirit and ideal of the chief Religious Orders of the Church.

THE JESUITS

By The Most Reverend Alban Goodier S.J.,
Archbishop of Hierapolis.

THE BENEDICTINES

By Dom David Knowles, O.S.B.

OTHER VOLUMES IN PREPARATION

CONTENTS

THE DOMINICANS

I

INTRODUCTION

To appreciate the distinctive character of any religious order it is necessary to understand how it came into being. This is particularly true of the Order of St. Dominic. Like all the other great orders it dates from a severe crisis in the history of Christianity. It was designed in an hour of peril to safeguard Christian institutions and traditions older than itself, and to infuse the spirit of Christianity into a new and undisciplined development of civilized society. From the first this very definite end was clearly understood and intended, and equally definite means were deliberately chosen for its achievement. No institution has ever remained more consistently faithful to its original plan and purpose. In the twentieth century the Order of Preachers still pursues the identical aims for which it was designed in the thirteenth; and except for a very few, very trivial changes—for which calculated provision was made at the beginning—it still employs the same means in the pursuit of those aims. This is not due to any cast-iron rigidity in the Order itself, for though very stable it is also very elastic. It is due rather to the fact that the developments of the thirteenth century are still vitally effective in civilized society; men are still constantly breaking away from the discipline of reason and of Christianity, and the oldest Christian institutions and traditions still need to be protected against their excesses. Hence within his cloister a Dominican of the twentieth century has little if anything to remind him that he is not actually living in the thirteenth; yet when his relations with the age he lives in are under discussion, so far is he from any suspicion of being behind the times that he has frequently to defend himself against the accusation of being in too great a hurry to get ahead of them.

Essentially, everything in the life of the Church is peculiarly her own. But the external developments of that life bear indelibly the stamp of the age in which each development occurred. The world in which the Church first began to be recognizable as a complete and organized society was predominantly Greek in its thought and its finer arts, and entirely

Roman in its practical affairs and material conditions. Hence the first developments of Christian theology and the oldest and noblest elements in the liturgy of the Church are cast for ever in a Grecian mould; her earliest practical developments—her geographical orientation, her system of laws, her administrative methods, her discipline, her official language, in a word all the fundamentals of her ordered and organized life generally—are Latin and Roman in every feature and every line. A very eminent modern statesman has said that if Christianity had not been transplanted at an early stage from its original Palestinian to its subsequent Roman setting it would have perished as inevitably and as quickly as any of the Levantine sects contemporary with its beginnings. This statement is obviously untrue: it stands condemned by reason and facts as well as by Catholic Faith. The Church has long ago satisfied the whole world that she is no parasite; history has proved again and again that her vitality is her own, and infinitely more enduring and fertile than any pagan civilization ever was or could be. Indeed it is entirely thanks to the supernatural agency of the Church that the influence, and even the memory, of Greece and Rome have survived to our day. It is quite conceivable that the earliest Christian developments might have followed other lines;

and even that the Church may yet one day be stripped as bare as she was on Calvary and afterwards emerge into new developments without a trace of anything Grecian or Roman in them. Nevertheless she cannot of her own accord recast the mould in which she has actually developed into a world-wide and fully organized society; nor can she suffer it to be disturbed without resisting almost as if she were struggling for her very existence. She is not merely supernatural; she is bound by the genuine laws of nature also. She could not, without great loss of time, of ground and of much labour—all which losses she naturally abhors—return to her primitive nakedness and begin again. Hence she clings to the precise forms into which she has developed very much as the soul clings to its particular body just as it is.

The Order of Preachers is very intimately connected with this process of historical development in the life of the Church. In the twelfth and thirteenth centuries a new civilization arose in Europe, partly in consequence of what the Church had already done for secular society, but more immediately as the result of purely natural causes, economic, social and political. Without sacrificing anything that she had assimilated from previous civilizations, the Church, through Pope and Councils, began to adapt herself to the new conditions, and to encourage all that was good in them by reproducing their counterpart within herself and out of her own resources. The immediate result of this development from within was the Order of Preachers. It is the distinction of that Order to have been conceived by the Church, brought into being by her, and formed out of her own substance. The mission which the Order holds from the Church is not in the nature of an appointment; it is the *raison d'être* of the Order, the purpose for which it was called into existence. No other Order is officially described in terms of its work: the title of "Friars Preachers" was not assumed by Dominicans to describe themselves, but carefully chosen for them by Pope Honorius III at the time the Order was founded.

Dominicans are readily distinguished from other religious by their distinctive habit, their particular customs, and many other external signs. But the distinctive character of the Order reaches far deeper than any of these things would suggest. It is the immediate result of the special relation in which the Order stands to the Church. In its creation the Church expressed, in a very deliberate and formal way, her own notes of Apostolicity and Catholicity. Hence amongst its most important characteristics is a temper at once conservative and progressive.

It is itself an outstanding example of the law of development at work in the life of the Church. It sums up in order the historic usages of the Christian centuries in a life which belongs emphatically to the present, though its thoughts are ever in the past and its concern is ever for the future. It clings tenaciously to all the traditions it embodies; yet it cannot endure that their development should stand still for a moment. In its own affairs, and in the work for which it was created by the Church, it has always shown a remarkable genius for the continuous development of old institutions, suitably to the needs of each succeeding age, and without the least disfigurement or mutilation of any growth that has preceded. It is the connecting link between the older monastic orders and the active orders later than itself in origin. It resumes in itself all the essential characteristics of the former, and anticipates all those of the latter. So true is this that it is difficult to express in a single sentence its own distinctive character, unless a paradox is permissible : for the Order of Preachers is distinguished amongst the orders of the Church by those characteristics which are common to all the rest.

All the Orders agree primarily in this, that they are immediately subject to the pope. The dependence of the Order of Preachers on the papacy is absolute. The popes called it into existence and defined its character and work. Its first principle of action has from the first been to look to the popes for inspiration and to wait for their initiative. Democratic in constitution and government, with power to make and unmake all its superiors, high and low, it has never attempted either in theory or in practice to treat with a pope on any other terms than simple obedience. In these days that does not seem very remarkable; but it must be remembered that the Dominican Order has lived through the days of the Great Schism and the Conciliar Theory. In those days, when the absolute authority of the popes was under debate, its great champions were Dominicans like St. Catherine of Siena and Blessed John Dominici. For centuries the Dominican Constitutions made no allusion to the absolute authority of the pope, and then it was introduced only in a parenthesis; and even still at his profession a Dominican promises obedience to God, the Blessed Virgin and the Master General of the Order, without any mention of the pope. That this silence means unquestioning consent to the doctrine as defined to-day is proved by something more than the consistent attitude of the Order. St. Thomas Aquinas in the thirteenth century taught that all religious were bound by their vow to obey the pope "not only in those matters that are common to all the faithful, but also in those that specially concern their religious life." He could not as a Dominican have taught otherwise; for every step by which his Order had moved into being and developed the character of which he is so perfect an example, was a direct act of obedience to an expressed wish of the Holy See. In action the conservative yet progressive temper of St. Dominic is indistinguishable from the Apostolicity and Catholicity of the papacy. He did not begin to found his Order until the great progressive pope then reigning had very distinctly called for it. His conservative inclination was merely seconding the conservatism of the same pope and a General Council, when, instead of building on new foundations, he established his Order under the Rule of St Augustine to which he himself was already bound.

II

THE CHURCH AND SOCIETY IN THE THIRTEENTH CENTURY

At the end of the twelfth century society in Western Europe was torn between two extreme and opposite tendencies, the one stubbornly conservative, the other riotously progressive. Feudalism, still immensely strong, was fighting with all its strength to maintain itself against the encroachments of a powerful popular movement among its former serfs, who were everywhere emancipating themselves and establishing themselves into independent communities in new towns and cities. Both parties were profoundly Christian, at least in sentiment, yet each in a different way was a menace to the faith of Christendom. Feudalism was closely identified with the traditions of the Christian centuries preceding, and clung to them tenaciously; but its Christian spirit was already dying, if not actually dead. The new democracy was willing enough to preserve the spirit of Christianity, but it was impatient of the

Christian traditions which it identified with its enemy; and its repudiation of those traditions implied a rejection of much that was essential to Christianity and enshrined in them.

Widely different in their origin, feudalism and Benedictine monasticism were intimately associated in their development, and each was profoundly influenced by the other. The germs of the feudal system can be seen already existing in the tribal laws and customs of the German barbarians of whom Cæsar and Tacitus wrote. Benedictine monasticism was a product of Roman Christianity. Both institutions began as a migration in pursuit of improved conditions of life; but both moved originally from opposite poles. The monks withdrew from civilized centres in search of peace. Taking with them the traditions of civilization they settled on land that none other coveted, cultivated it and prospered on it. The more they scattered themselves the more their isolated settlements expanded, and were held together by spiritual bonds in the unity of a common civilization. The barbarians usurped civilized territory, fighting barbarously, first to possess it, then to hold it in parcels against one another. The more they united for war, the more they were divided in the peace that followed. The example of the monks gradually converted them to Christianity. Immediately the two institutions began to react powerfully upon one another. Simple natural causes, social, economic and political, enabled the independent lay communities to conform more and more to the example of the monasteries. Slavery disappeared, and the simple division of men personally free into superiors and subjects became more and more strongly marked. Legally, and in practice also, except in matters purely personal and religious, the relation between a lay lord and his subjects was assimilated to that already existing between an abbot and his monks. Abbot and lay lord alike were sole masters of the community over which they ruled. Each had his officials and his court, and independently of all save the highest religious authority administered justice at will and held his position for life. The serf like the monk was bound to his lord by an oath, and immovable from the soil on which he was sworn to labour. The only difference that remained arose from the temporal ambitions of lay society as opposed to the spiritual aims of monasticism; and even this difference disappeared, with pitiful disorders in both cases, wherever pure spiritual enthusiasm declined. The avowed object of feudal society was the possession and enjoyment of land, and its ultimate appeal in the pursuit of this object was avowedly to force. In theory, and for the most part in practice also, the monk was a subject by his own free but irrevocable choice. He willingly divested himself of all rights, and undertook as a duty whatever his superior might exact. By profession a slave, by common consent he was free; his personal dignity, therefore, remained intact. In lay society subjects were made subject by force of circumstances, and kept in subjection by force of arms. The notion of the liberty of subjects survived more effectively in England than elsewhere; yet even here feudal law, unless it was mitigated by the policy and favour of kings, conceded no rights but only duties to burgesses and villeins; and feudal conditions tended to suppress the lower orders of freemen into one or other of these classes. Mere personal freedom, though it might carry with it, at least in England, certain customary rights and precarious opportunities of accumulating personal wealth, was of itself no title to either legal or social franchise. Legal and social freedom belonged not to persons, but to personages; that is, to proprietors of land, which alone conferred a title in law. Villein and burgher, under pain of becoming outlaws, were both obliged to do homage, that is hand over their manhood to their lord: in peace the former tilling his lands, the latter making his armour, building and provisioning his castle; in war both defending his possessions with their lives.

The fusion of monks and lay communities in one society produced what now we call Western Christendom: the union of a vast congregation of Christians under a common language, a common social structure, common economic conditions, common political and military aims and institutions. Some of these bonds were never perfectly realized except as ideals; but some of them were actually achieved in practice. The common social structure and economic conditions were very thoroughly worked out, even to the detriment of religion, which was the first principle making for unity and order. So true is this that the later history of the monasteries is a more constant witness to the working of economic and social laws than to that of the religious laws which first produced them. Generally speaking the social and economic, and even the political, influence of feudalism on the monasteries and the whole organization of the Church was greater than the purely religious influence of the latter on feudalism. The monks as landowners became social personages. The monastic lands became the chief sources of wealth. Abbots became temporal rulers, controlling the services of burgesses and villeins, equipping them for war, administering justice to them in their courts, minting coinage for their use. The same process of feudalization extended itself to the rest of the clergy. The Church was as zealous for their admission into European society as that society was to absorb them. Legally it could only recognize them as outlaws, or as serfs, or as landowning personages. That they should be the last was as necessary in the eyes of the Church as it was desirable for society, which required their sanction for its laws. Hence the equal enthusiasm of the Church to receive and of the State to grant ecclesiastical benefices in the form of territorial possessions and feudal rights. By common consent bishops ranked with abbots and barons as feudal lords; and because of their closer organization they became the most powerful body of all. Following their example, but again with a temporal instead of a spiritual aim, material necessity being always the principal motive for submission, the lay lords began to arrange themselves into centralized and subordinated groups. More and more from the ninth to the thirteenth century, there is a growing enthusiasm among clergy and laity alike, with the voice of individual ambition alone dissenting, for the incorporation of every human interest into one religious and civil society, with the pope and clergy leading the way not by preaching religion pure and simple, but by exemplifying it in all the highest offices of society.

All that can be said against such an ideal is

that it expected too much of human nature. It failed, first because not all the popes were as great as Gregory VII and Innocent III, nor all the bishops like St. Anselm and St. Thomas of Canterbury; and secondly because feudalism, in spite of having become Christian and absorbed the clergy, never outgrew the barbarian lust for fat lands to which it owed its origin.

The failure led to religious and civil disorders, and both were most serious in the clergy. Monastic life and the cure of souls became an object of secular ambition for the sake of the wealth and social status that went with them. As the material cares and attachments of the clergy increased, their religious character was coarsened, their spiritual authority weakened and despised. Learning decayed, morals deteriorated, religion was often reduced either to shameless hypocrisy or to an ignorant and superstitious sentiment. In a society which safeguarded rights only by insisting on duties, the lapse of the clergy from a sense of their principal duty had terrible consequences. Free rein was given to the tendency of every man to insist on the duty of others, and neglect his own; to press his advantage over his subjects in his own interest. England, always on the whole more fortunate than other countries, supplies a painful enough example of the evils that followed. Only a strong ruler could keep order, and that by force alone. The kings allied themselves with the lower classes to keep the barons and baronial clergy in subjection. When in the days of Stephen the crown was powerless, there ensued the sheer anarchy that was so much more common on the continent. The barons throw off all restraint. They play the tyrant on their own estates, conduct private wars, league together in inconstant unions, each seeking his own advantage and his neighbour's ruin. Each one multiplies castles, mints his own coinage, abuses his judicial powers to bend all his subjects cruelly to his will. In this English example, fortunately, the clergy were sound enough to intervene at last and save the country from depopulation and bankruptcy. But elsewhere, especially in the South of France, the clergy were often the worst offenders, in their own temporal interests fomenting religious and civil disorders, and fighting with both spiritual and military weapons, now as Crusaders under the standard of the Cross, now as private marauders in secret league against it.

These political evils inevitably aroused a spirit of revolt amongst the oppressed populations of the towns and rural estates. In the revolution that followed much blood was shed throughout Europe, the English people making much more peaceful progress than others. During the twelfth century the burgesses of the towns, favoured everywhere by economic developments and here in England by royal charters, were beginning to emancipate themselves from their absolute dependence on the castle, abbey or cathedral, under whose walls they had lived in conditions as abject as the rural serfs, excepting only the isolation and the unskilled labour which forbade the latter such opportunities of acquiring political experience and wealth as came the way of the more densely packed artisans and tradesfolk of the towns. These latter won the privilege of paying their feudal dues in money raised corporately, instead of in personal services and individual levies in kind. They thus became corporations with powers of contract. Their numbers grew partly by natural increase, partly by the addition of fugitive serfs from the country. In England, for the villein who remained in them unclaimed for a year and a day the chartered towns won the right of freedom in perpetuity. Elsewhere towns had usually to fight for their independence; they therefore welcomed every able-bodied recruit as an accession to their own forces and a weakening of their enemies. In intervals of peace, once they had bought exemption from military and other services, the townsmen were more profitably employed than their former masters, who, with the exception of the more exemplary monks, had no other trade but war and no other pastime but the chase. The craftsmen began to improve their skill and their industrial organization, and so to increase the output of valuables that called for markets. Their free use of money as taxpayers qualified them to become traders, first on a small scale locally, then internationally as merchants, bankers, and respected creditors of popes and kings.

Thus existing towns developed rapidly and new ones appeared everywhere. Their growth, though full of promise to everyone economically, at first excited the strongest prejudice amongst the landlords, who saw the power of the purse being gradually transferred to the hands of a class they despised and their own signorial authority weakened in consequence. The clergy as a body were the bitterest enemies of the new urban populations and the very last to become reconciled to their success and aspirations; and that not merely because they clung tenaciously to their temporal power, but because, being profoundly conservative, and attached by all their best instincts to the ideas of an earlier age, they considered temporal advantages and exemptions to be a necessary condition of their spiritual influence. To many of them, and especially to the more pious, it must have seemed a sinful disloyalty to allow such an encroachment on Church property and ecclesiastical privileges as was often entailed in the emancipation of their own dependents, with its consequent treaties, bargains and quarrels respecting rights and territories. The saints of the period, though always friendly to the landless people and full of compassion when their lot was hard, were much more earnest to encourage them in their duties than to tolerate an examination of their rights, or to favour an assertion of them. No help came even from the monasteries, though sympathy at least might have been expected when monks of the better type were so often having worldly-minded abbots imposed upon them. Monastic reforms there were in plenty, and brilliant ones, in the tenth and eleventh centuries; but these had not touched the evils of society, for they one and all took the form of a more rigorous retirement from the world, and far from repudiating the social and economic advantages which the age accorded to ecclesiastics, they set themselves to justify these by being worthy of them. St. Bernard is the best exponent of the highest monastic ideals of his time. The rights of subjects is a notion with which he has no patience at all. The only rights he recognizes are those of God and His Church, and such as these have sanctioned in times past. His powerful preaching is all an insistence on the perfect performance of duties. In the intellectual renaissance of the eleventh century, which was a resurrection of classical authorities, the monks led the way by becoming schoolmasters and opening their monastic schools to external pupils. In the scholastic awakening of speculation in the twelfth century, when Abelard and others less suspect began to advocate liberty and analyse the notion of rights, the monasteries one after another closed their schools to external scholars and secular learning, giving as their reason that logic was unsuited to men who had left the world for the kingdom of heaven's sake.

Thus from the very first, and on almost every ground, the clergy and the new population of artisans and merchants were hostile to one another. At the same time the spiritual needs of the new citizen class were very great; so, too, was its power for good or evil. Steeped in Christian traditions and schooled for generations under the discipline of unremitting labour, poverty, suffering and exceedingly harsh laws, it was piously and even ascetically inclined, and on the whole very much less corrupt than its former masters, clerical and lay. New to freedom and wealth won by its own efforts, it was light-hearted and intelligent, ambitious, enterprising and industrious. It was intensely interested in its own political status, organization, and government, in all of which its tendencies were naturally democratic. Life in its growing towns was noisy and quarrelsome; everyone was eager to learn and everyone had some new information to impart, some new theory to propound. Anyone able to say anything worth hearing could confidently stand up in the streets and be sure of an eager audience and searching questions. As always happens in the days of a popular awakening, the topics most keenly discussed were the elements of philosophy and religion. Teachers with any pretensions to authority in such matters were everywhere welcome and easily secured enthusiastic adherents. Many stepped forward into the arena, but in spite of the appeals of Innocent III, and in spite of his direct commission to the Cistercians and his modifications of their rule against preaching, no successful exponents of official Catholic teaching appeared until St. Dominic and his companions entered the lists. They, when they came, encouraged all manner of questions and gave answers as completely satisfactory as only Christian answers can be. Their principal duty was the positive exposition of Christian doctrine; but often before they could come to that they had to expend much time and labour in refuting answers to current difficulties that had already been given from other than orthodox Christian sources. Moorish and Jewish traders from Spain, and camp-followers from the eastern Crusades had long been spreading hints and scraps of Arabian philosophy in all the new towns to which they came; and very early in the twelfth century it began to be rumoured everywhere that long before Christianity was heard of Aristotle had solved all the problems of human society. Two powerful religious sects, the one very ancient and of pagan origin, the other only recently detached from the Church, had been so busily disseminating their heresies in Lombardy and Languedoc as to be very strongly established in practically every city of those two populous provinces. It was actual contact with one of these that first brought St. Dominic out into the open as a preacher and religious reformer.

This was the sect of the Cathari or Albigenses. It was lineally descended from the Manichæan Dualists who first appeared in Persia in the third century, and became so powerful in North Africa in the fourth and fifth. The doctrines refuted by St. Augustine had survived, with superficial variations and accretions, for over a thousand years, principally in the Balkans. Thence they passed, first into the North of Italy, and then into the South of France where, favoured by long-standing Jewish and Mahommedan influences and the apathy of the Catholic clergy, they struck deep roots among the laity of all classes. According to this teaching everything in existence proceeded from one of two first principles which were respectively good and evil. The evil principle, they maintained, was the source of all matter; therefore the human body was evil, and a good life consisted in the rigorous mortification of all its natural appetites. They especially condemned the eating of flesh meat, marriage, and the procreation of children. These doctrines were everywhere preached, with many arguments and much show of learning, by an inner circle of adherents, known as the "perfect", who practised, or affected to practise, a very strict poverty and other austerities.

The other great sect was that of the Waldensians. It originated amongst the pious laity of Lyons in the latter half of the twelfth century. These laymen were merchants who wished to restore Christianity to the simplicity of apostolic times. Their attempts to preach reform within the Church brought them into conflict with the clergy. They went into schism and began a reformed religion of their own, teaching that the Church had abandoned her mission and forfeited all claims to respect and obedience.

The seriousness of all these complicated problems was a matter of deep anxiety to the great Pope Innocent III. From the beginning of his pontificate, with characteristic energy and insight, he set himself to deal with them. He addressed himself with much sympathy to the heretics, recognizing that the laxity of the clergy was largely responsible for their defection. He appealed to them as their father to return to the obedience they owed him, and made the way easy for them, by allowing converts to retain all their former customs which were not inconsistent with Catholic Faith.

In spite of strong episcopal prejudice he allowed groups of them to form themselves into religious Orders and preach against the heresy they had renounced. To recall the clergy to their true vocation he addressed admonitions to individual bishops and began to convene the fourth Lateran Council. His special aim in all his ecclesiastical reforms was to restore to the Church the lost art of preaching, and to qualify the clergy for it by a revival of apostolic zeal, of the virtues proper to their state, and of ecclesiastical learning.

In response to his appeal there soon came forward two great saints—two men of very different character and antecedents: Dominic Guzman, cleric, and Francis of Assisi, layman. Francis leapt up from the heart of the new people of the cities, and full of their gay spirit led them singing to a more romantic adventure and a more arduous enterprise than had hitherto suggested itself to their wildest and most generous dreams. The movement he led was so exuberant that had it not been providentially safeguarded it must inevitably have run into excesses and so added to the evils of the time. Fortunately for Francis the same Providence that inspired him had long been preparing Dominic to anticipate his glorious outburst of asceticism and mysticism. Before Francis left his father's home Dominic had already begun his apostolic work: he had quietly walked out of the old world that seemed to be passing away—the world of feudalism, monasticism and conservative ecclesiastical traditions. He was the son of a Castilian feudal lord; as a boy he had been trained by clerical schoolmasters, and since early manhood he had lived in cloistral seclusion as a regular canon, one of a cathedral chapter. His mind and character had been formed under those very institutions and according to those very traditions which were now in danger of becoming effete; and he was as deeply attached to them all as men like Francis were afraid of them all. At the very first encounter with the new people of the French towns Dominic found himself as closely in sympathy with the serious side of their natural character as Francis was with the lighter side of life in Umbria. The two men, being equally saints, were at one with the ambitious spirit and the ascetic temper of the new generation. What distinguished Dominic was his eager sympathy with the more intellectual side of its young life: its habit of asking questions, its readiness to learn and to be taught, its zeal for constructive social order, for democratic freedom and responsibility, for representative government, and with all this, for a centralized authority which would keep society united and stable, and at the same time progressive. He successfully undertook to show the new civilization that the Church, and the Church alone, could satisfy these legitimate aspirations; and that not by a root and branch reform, but by an easy evolution of the life already implicit in her existing institutions.

III

THE VOCATION OF ST. DOMINIC

Saint Dominic was born in 1170 at Calaruega in Old Castille. His father was a pious nobleman, and his mother, Joanna of Aza, has been declared Blessed by the Church. Dominic was the youngest of three sons. He was educated, first at home, then by a clerical relative of his mother, and finally at Palencia where there was a school which later became a famous university, the fore-runner of Salamanca. In his twenty-fourth year or thereabouts he was ordained priest and being already a canon in the cathedral chapter of Osma, his native diocese, went to take up his duties there. About the time he joined it the chapter was reformed; its members became regular Augustinian canons. Dominic was soon appointed sub-prior and later prior. Such glimpses as we have of his character during these early years reveal all those qualities which stamped themselves on his later work: a studious and well disciplined mind, an iron will tempered with sympathy for the misfortunes of others, a talent for leadership and government, a deep and virile piety.

While he was Prior of Osma he accompanied his bishop, Diego, on a diplomatic mission to Denmark. Two journeys, twice backwards and forwards, had to be made. Thus Dominic passed several times through Languedoc, where the Albigensian heresy was rampant. It is on record that he sat up the whole of one night expounding the Catholic Faith to the landlord of the inn where he and the bishop were staying, and by morning had converted him from his heresy. The story is very significant when it is remembered that, in theory at least, the heretics denounced as evil all those bodily comforts which inn-keepers supply to others in order to live well themselves.

Their diplomatic mission concluded, the bishop made a pilgrimage to Rome with the intention of resigning his see and going to preach the gospel to the Cumans, heathen Tartars inhabiting the basins of the Volga and the Dnieper. Dominic went with him, he, too, bent on devoting himself to the conversion of the Cumans. This was late in 1204.

For the pope, Innocent III, it was an unusual and agreeable experience to receive from a bishop such a request as Diego addressed to him. In this case, however, it probably did not altogether surprise him, for he must have known that this bishop had been prior, and his companion sub-prior, of the chapter which had applied to him in 1199 for permission to establish itself as a regular community of Austin canons. On that occasion he had written to Osma cordially acceding to their request. On this occasion he gave their request an equally cordial welcome, but did not grant it. Instead he sent them both to labour for the conversion of Languedoc.

By his orders they went first to Cîteaux. A year earlier he had appointed two Cistercian monks his legates in Languedoc, to protect Catholic interests there. When they reported that they could do nothing in face of the indifference, and in some cases the open opposition, of the bishops and lay lords, Innocent called on the Abbot of Cîteaux to select from amongst his monks a body of preachers to support the legates. In a letter of 31st May, 1204, confirming the election of a new abbot, Arnaud Amaury, he appointed the latter to be head of the legation.

The Cistercians had not begun to achieve anything when Diego and Dominic appeared in Rome. The work the monks had been given was exceedingly difficult and they were not ideally fitted for it. The Abbot-General had too many monasteries under his care to be able to devote to the problems in Languedoc the attention they required. His monks were not only unaccustomed to preaching, they were positively disqualified for it by their best traditions as enclosed contemplatives, and had been expressly forbidden by St. Bernard to engage in it. Moreover, in their progress through the disaffected province they observed all the state and magnificence which was the ecclesiastical custom everywhere at the time, and so aroused against themselves one of the strongest prejudices of the heretics they were sent to reconcile.

Thus the papal injunctions lay heavily on the monks of Cîteaux when Diego and Dominic arrived there. These two put new heart into them by their announcement that they would now lead the way in the more difficult matter of preaching and establishing friendly relations with the heretics. To avoid all suspicion of rivalry, and to temper his criticisms of the way things were being done, Diego had himself formally clothed in the Cistercian habit.

From Cîteaux the two new missionaries went to Montpellier, where they presented themselves to the three legates. They found them almost in despair. The bishops and baron were hindering or opposing them at every turn Diego urged an entirely new plan of campaign. He proposed that instead of depending on the authority of the bishops and the military aid of the barons, as they had done hitherto, they should now appeal directly to the heretics, addressing their preaching to them and winning them by their example. The example he advocated was that of Christ and His Apostles: the strictest poverty and simplicity of life, open-air preaching, and public disputations with heretical teachers whenever these threw out a challenge.

At first the legates hesitated to adopt the suggestion. It seemed so novel, and so great a concession to heretical practice and criticisms, that they feared lest it should alienate even such Catholics as were well disposed. They feared, too, that apostolic poverty would not only hamper their freedom of movement and action, but that it would also diminish their authority in the eyes of the great personages with whom they had to deal on behalf of the pope. As for mendicancy, that was forbidden to the clergy by Canon Law. But the zeal of the legates for the cause entrusted to them was sincere; they could not long withstand the arguments and the example of Diego and his companion. They went as far as they dared to follow the bishop's lead. Dismissing their long cavalcade of retainers and servants, they set out on foot from Montpellier, visiting one heretical stronghold after another and preaching the Catholic

Faith in all the towns and villages through which they passed. At first the little band of missionaries held together and prospered. Their success encouraged the abbots of a dozen other Cistercian abbeys to rally, with a large following of monks, to the support of their brethren of Cîteaux. Fulke, a Cistercian, lately made Bishop of Toulouse, became the ardent patron of the mission and remained the champion of its leaders all his life. It was subsequently from him, and in his cathedral city, that the Order of Preachers received its first charter and its first home. It emerged very rapidly and very distinctly from the large body of Cistercians now in the field. This large body was split up into small groups, to each of which was assigned a district. Thrown once more upon their own resources the monks again found their work as preachers uncongenial and unfruitful. They retired to their cloisters, leaving Diego and Dominic to carry on the mission with a mere handful of young companions.

To recruit their forces Diego returned to Osma, where he died shortly after his arrival. Thus Dominic, a simple canon, was left to preach the mission without the authority and protection of his bishop. This position was uncanonical, for preaching was the exclusive province of bishops, and neither custom nor canon law favoured any ample delegation of their power to the lesser clergy. Bishop Fulke of Toulouse, in whose diocese Dominic was, did all in his power to help him in his work. He gave him the Church of Notre Dame at Prouille and sanctioned his foundation of a convent of enclosed women there, thus inaugurating what is now known as the Second Order. To have given Dominic and his companions an official position as preachers in his own diocese would have been to lay the foundations of the First Order also. It would have been only natural to have done that first, and subsequent events prove that Fulke recognized this and would gladly have done it at once had he considered it within his authority. But he evidently thought the establishment of Prouille as much as it was permissible for him to attempt. The name *Sancta Praedicatio*, by which this foundation was first known, seems to imply fairly clearly that from the beginning it was intended to give Dominic at least an unofficial standing as an approved preacher in the diocese.

Fully official approval was not long delayed. One of the legates explained the situation to Innocent III and asked what was to be done. The pope replied in a letter of 17th November, 1206, which marks an epoch in the history of religious orders. The legate was peremptorily ordered to exert all his powers to further apostolic preaching by men suited for the work.

There is no mention of Dominic by name; the letter is, therefore, not in any sense a charter formally approving the foundation of his Order. But it brings such a foundation well within the bounds of practicable ecclesiastical politics; and if it did not actually inspire St. Dominic with his first definite idea of establishing a new religious order in the Church, it certainly set the seal of authority on whatever ambitions he had already conceived in that direction. Taken together with all that had preceded, this letter leaves us wondering whether it was in the mind of Dominic, or of Diego, or of Innocent himself that the idea of an apostolic order of preachers was first conceived. When the pope describes the kind of preachers and preaching he requires the legate to provide, he draws a very accurate picture of the character of Diego and Dominic and of the way in which they had conducted their life and their missionary work hitherto. In Dominican history this letter is something much more important than the endorsement by a great pope of St. Dominic's ideals; it is the voice of supreme authority proposing those ideals without acknowledging anyone but the Holy Ghost as their Author; and more even than that it is a definite command to the right men, whoever they may be, to put those ideals into immediate execution. Every religious order rightly treasures the credentials that prove it to be the creation of something infinitely higher than human ambition. The Dominican Order is singularly fortunate to possess in documentary form this authentic proof that its members "*non ex sanguinibus, neque ex voluntate carnis, neque ex voluntate viri, sed ex Deo nati sunt*".

With this encouragement from the pope, and with the cordial support of Fulke, Dominic spent eight years labouring by word and example for the conversion of Catholics and heretics alike to purity of Christian faith and practice. Without official canonical status as yet, he was qualifying for it in fact, and probably in intention also. In 1208 one of the papal legates was assassinated by the heretics. Provoked by this, Innocent sanctioned an armed crusade against them. Dominic followed the crusaders into the field preaching in both camps the same gospel of peace and forbearance. His own life was closely modelled on that of Christ and His Apostles as described in the New Testament, and his favourite reading was the Epistles of St. Paul and the Conferences of Cassian. To recall the heretics to submission to the pope, and the orthodox to their duty as Catholics, he appealed directly to these documentary evidences of primitive Christianity.

His success was complete. The crusaders overcame the heretics in the field, and attributed their success in arms to Dominic's spiritual conquest of themselves and his inroads into the heresy that had united and strengthened their adversaries against them. Simon de Montfort, whose son later reformed the English Parliament, was at the head of the Catholic forces. He became the close friend and patron of Dominic, and assisted him materially in the foundation at Prouille which, throughout these years, was the primary concern of his constructive and administrative talents. Others, bishops, barons and private individuals, shared the enthusiasm of de Montfort, and added their gifts to his. But his most devoted admirers were to be found amongst the great numbers of converts whom he had by his immediate personal influence reclaimed from heresy. He was several times nominated to vacant bishoprics. The resolution with which he refused all such offers, favourable though they were to his work as a preacher and spiritual reformer, shows how clearly he had already defined in his own mind the ideal of a universal apostolate unrestricted by diocesan boundaries and reponsibilities.

It was at this very moment, the beginning of 1215, that Fulke formally appointed Dominic and his companions to be his official preachers in the diocese of Toulouse. In so doing he clearly did not intend to limit their activities to a single diocese. By the manner of his appointment, by the style in which he describes his new relation with Dominic, and by the line of action he immediately pursues, Fulke makes it very obvious that he is not merely providing for the needs of his own diocese, but that he is introducing to the whole Church men eminently capable of doing the work which the pope so long ago called upon all the bishops to promote, and which none of them have so far been able to inaugurate for want of suitable workers. It may even be that in all this Fulke was executing the direct commands of the pope; for there are many signs that the latter had long before planned a universal mission for Dominic when he should have finished the work in Languedoc to which he and Diego had been sent from Rome. Innocent himself, it will be remembered, had given them that mission, imposing it on them in preference to another of their own choice. Although there is no explicit documentary proof of the fact, it is more than likely that he followed the fortunes of Dominic in Languedoc from start to finish with the closest interest. The work the saint was commissioned to do there differed only by being more urgent, from the work which the great pope wished to have done throughout the whole Church. Innocent's hopes for the whole work as well as for the most urgent part of it cannot but have centred on the only competent men who, in the whole course of his pontificate, volunteered their services as missionaries, gladly yielded their own preferences to his requirements, and proved themselves more and more as time went on to be ideally suited to the work of reform by preaching and example on which he had set his heart from the beginning of his reign. At any rate, whatever the truth of the matter may be, one of the most important characteristics of the Dominican Order is admirably illustrated by the fact that Dominican historians are not only willing, but eager, to rob their revered Founder of the honour of sole authorship at every step of his foundation in order to credit the initiative as fully as possible to a pope.

The circumstances of St. Dominic's appointment to be official preacher in the diocese of Toulouse all point to an immediate purpose aimed beyond the confines of that diocese and transcending its individual needs. Fulke assisted at a provincial council which assembled at Montpellier in January 1213, as soon as the armed crusade against the Albigensians was successfully concluded. He returned to his see accompanied by the papal legate who had presided there. His appointment of Dominic was made under the eyes of the legate. It was evidently intended as a first step towards fulfilling the injunctions of the council, and especially its demands for the reform of the clergy, which Innocent, recommending the methods employed by Dominic, had years before imposed on the legates as one of their special duties. The official act by which Dominic is now appointed repeats the substance, and recalls the wording, of the papal letter of 17th November, 1206. The preachers are to extirpate heresy; to combat vice, to teach the rule of faith, and to reform morals. The means approved for this end are preaching and evangelical poverty. It is distinctly laid down that the preachers shall make their journeys on foot. They are granted a share of ecclesiastical tithes, with the condition that whatever of this remains at the end of each year after their needs have been supplied is to be returned. It was understood that books were to be among the first of the necessaries for which this revenue was to be used. The brethren were now established in a house of their own in Toulouse, the handsome gift of a citizen who soon afterwards joined them himself.

The newly established community, about seven in number, at once proved its appreciation of its enlarged responsibilities. In compliance with the decrees of the Third Lateran Council which Innocent III had frequently reiterated, Fulke had re-established his cathedral school, appointing as Master of Theology Alexander of Stavensby, an Englishman, who later, as Bishop of Lichfield, proved a staunch friend of the English Dominican Province. To him now as pupils went Dominic, aged forty-three, and his young companions. Hitherto it has been his duty to combat the errors of heretics and the moral laxity of believers. For that it has been enough to propose by word and example the fruits of his own meditations on the Scriptures and other Christian documents. Now he is appointed an official exponent of positive Catholic doctrine. For this the reasons that are enough to confound heresy and reprove sinners will not suffice. Therefore he begins his new work not from the starting point of reason, but from the authoritative teaching of the Church. He goes to school to learn the traditional teaching of Christianity exactly as it existed in his day. When he resumes his work, reason will have ample play once more, but it will have a secondary function, not the primary one that falls to it when truth is being proposed to those whose faith is weak, or who have no faith at all. This return of St. Dominic to school in middle age admirably illustrates the traditional Dominican conception, so often enlarged upon by St. Thomas, of the relation between reason and faith, between philosophy and theology.

With the canonical establishment of Dominic and his companions in the diocese of Toulouse the life of the Order of Preachers has virtually begun and the principal traits of its character are already distinguishable. Very much, it is true, still remains to be done before it can strictly be called a religious order; it has yet to elaborate a religious rule of life peculiar to itself, to obtain from Rome a formal approval of this and a world-wide mission, to spread itself abroad, and to develop within itself a system of government that will ensure its remaining an order in fact as well as in name as it spreads across the world and down the centuries. In the eight years of life that still remain to him its founder will have much to do to achieve all that. He did it in fact with astonishing vigour and thoroughness. Those years are the most spectacular of his life, and our information about his movements during them is not only more detailed, it is greater in sum than all our information about him during the forty and more years of his previous history. But already as we see him in 1213 we are able to discern what manner of man he is; and to know that is to understand all that matters most in the Order he founded. The history of the years that follow in the case of the one, of the centuries that are still unfolding themselves in the case of the other, is merely a filling in of outlines already visible and, because of their strong simplicity, no less impressive than the completed picture.

From one of his spiritual daughters we have a naive description of his outward appearance. "The blessed Dominic was of middle height and slender in build. He had a beautiful countenance with a rather sanguine complexion, ruddy-brown hair and beard, and beautiful eyes. A kind of glory shone from his brows which inspired all with respect and affection. He was always smiling and joyous, except when moved to compassion by the distress of another. He had long and elegant hands. His voice was full, musical and resonant. He never became bald, and the circle of hair on his tonsured head remained unbroken, touched with grey here and there." It is a picture of a soul rather than a body, and as such it describes not only St. Dominic, but the youthful freshness and the spiritual charm pervading even the flesh that has been so often remarked in so many of his sons. Needless to say, a prepossessing exterior is not a necessary qualification for membership of his Order; nevertheless, bodily grace has always been frankly appreciated there both as being commonly a witness to more precious graces within, and as being always a powerful aid to the graceful art of preaching in all its manifold forms. As for cultured grace in movement, speech, dress, and whatever else proceeds from the soul through the body or is reached by the soul through the body, these are obviously called for by the very nature of the Order. Its vocation is at once exemplary and formal. The call which St. Dominic answered was an appeal for men suited to preach the truth and beauty of Catholic faith and morals by word and example. The work of preaching by word has created a Dominican tradition of formal habits of thought, and consequently of words and actions. Form implies beauty, and unless it is lifeless and untrue—in which case it would be the perversion we all abhor as empty and meaningless formalism—it inevitably expresses itself in beauty of word and action. To preach by example the beauty of faith, and still more of morals, means to be exemplary in every possible way. It means not only to be a perfect example of both, but to make everything under one's control a perfect example of both. A contemporary describing St. Dominic's preaching says that "he abounded in examples." The nun's account of him just quoted authorizes us in reading this widely enough to mean that he made an example of everything that God had given him, so as to provide the best example he could of the beauty of the invisible things of faith.

Hence springs the formal yet natural beauty

that runs through the whole of Dominican life. To the public eye this is conspicuous in such diverse things as St. Thomas's Eucharistic hymns, the *Salve* procession at Compline, the habit, the paintings of Fra Angelico, the Dominican manuscripts of the thirteenth and following centuries. But seen from within and in its proper setting every detail is stamped with the same beauty. Educated under such influences the individual friar who did not cultivate all he could of natural grace in deportment, mind, and character, would inevitably be ill at ease himself and a distraction to others.

The official ecclesiastical documents of this period begin to indulge in vivid character sketches of the men the Church is looking for to renew the decaying faith and morals of the time. These may have been prophetic, and the truest praise of Dominic and his followers may simply be that they answered perfectly to the most sanguine hopes of contemporary Christian idealism. It is much more probable, however, that the popes and bishops who write these glowing sentences are merely describing the man, Dominic, whom they have already seen and heard, and are proposing him as a model to all other men of good will. Wherever he goes, to Rome, to Toulouse, to Paris, to Bologna, his appearance there is immediately followed by the publication, under the seal of the highest authorities, of documents full of references to "men suited to preach the gospel by word and example; imitating the poverty of Christ, humbly clad, travelling on foot from place to place . . . men powerful in word and work . . . champions of the faith and true lights of the world . . . invincible athletes of Christ."

In the final confirmation of the Order Honorius III expressly tells the Friars Preachers in the hearing of all the Church that this is the sort of men they are now ordained to be; and in a long series of documents immediately following they are so often and so explicitly described and praised as being such men that the phrases become consecrated to them, and are used both within the Order and outside it to define their special vocation. When in 1206 Innocent III begins to use such language he does not apply it expressly to Dominic, and, probable though it seems, we cannot be certain that he intends it to describe him as he already knows him. But whether so intended or not, it obviously does describe very pithily those characteristics which bound Diego and Dominic together, recommended them both to Innocent as ideal apostles for Languedoc, overcame there the obstinacy of heretics and the apathy of Catholics, won the warm patronage of Fulke, gathered his first companions around him, and finally became stamped on his Order as the character it inherited from him and was born to perpetuate.

"Powerful in word and work, and so suited to preach the gospel by word and example." These phrases are the first to be heard and the most frequently repeated. They sound the key-note in the character of Dominic and his foundation. His "suitability" was the result partly of a richly endowed nature, partly of a long and careful training under the full discipline that grace has established in Christian civilization—a Catholic home, Catholic schools, a cloistered life and a religious rule. In his Order natural gifts are as necessary, brilliant natural gifts as becoming as they were in his case. The gifts that were most conspicuous in him have always been the most conspicuous in his Order, and must always remain so as long as it worthily perpetuates his name and prospers in the vocation he has bequeathed to it.

Our glimpses of him in early youth reveal a serious mind delicately balanced by a heart full of feeling. At Palencia he sold his books to relieve the distressful poverty of others. Nature disposed him to be "powerful in word and work" All contemporary witnesses agree that he had a rare natural gift of eloquence: a voice full, pleasant to the ear, resounding; an imagination teeming with images; an attractive presence; the magnetic appeal of intelligent sympathy with his listeners. Long years of practice must have made him a very accomplished preacher. But in his preaching, as in the pulpit traditions he has left behind him, accomplishments would only hinder, and not help at all, if they were studied for their own sake. They flow unconsciously from the harmonious co-operation of a suitable head and heart and body.

The quality of his mind may be judged from the nature of the heresy with which he was the first to deal triumphantly. The Albigensians were in error on very profound matters: the absolute nature and universal causality of God; the goodness of all being; the problem of evil; the relation of body and soul in man. The mind of St. Dominic, and the Dominican mind generally, is best described as one that is naturally interested in these very questions as fundamental to an intelligent appreciation of all truth, and capable of answering them to the satisfaction of all minds great and small. St. Dominic for all his personal magnetism did not coax the Provençal heretics into the Catholic Church; he argued them into it. His first successes were all won hardly by discussion after discussion, in which he was pitted against the most powerful brains by which this very metaphysical heresy was served. Until he had won all along the line his gift of sympathy could only help him by making him patient in discussion with minds unequal to his own. His powers of persuasion were useless except to move converts and Catholics whose hearts were lagging behind their heads. With these he was persuasive, not by a weak condescension to the pious arguments at which logic laughs, but by the irresistible strength of example.

It is that example which shows us his heart in action, and enables us to see what kind of heart is most suitable for the Dominican vocation. Its most spectacular quality is courage. Popes acclaim him as an "athlete" and a "champion" (more literally rendered, a "pugilist"). Life in Spain is too easy for him. He wants to go to the banks of the Volga and fight the wild lawlessness for which the Tartar's name is still a proverb in our day. For a man of his mettle the pope has an even more arduous adventure to propose. He suggests Languedoc where at the moment no Catholic dared move abroad except sword in hand. Dominic goes there and stays there, and never girds on a sword. He attacks with words a noisy enemy whose language already differs from his own Castilian, and whose thoughts are as strange to him as his feudal and monastic traditions are hateful to them. They are fanatics and libertines by turns; he attacks them with an example of light-hearted austerity. More courageous even than that, he dares to be a thorough-going

Christian in courts and camps which are Christian in name and nothing else. And he proves himself an "invincible athlete" everywhere.

The secret of his courage and of all his other great qualities of heart is a very simple one. He is naturally a lover of his fellow men, and a believer in human nature. This natural virtue disposes him to follow Christ to the point of loving his enemies as much as himself. He is entirely free from all narrowness whether of race or class or sect, or any other of the divisions into which self-love groups men to make them bigots and enemies of their own kind. He relies on his simple manhood to subdue those against whom the pomp and armed power of great personages are of no avail. He had as little use for what those days called personage as for what these days call personality: he was just a plain person, nothing more and nothing less. He reminded the world of the lesson Christ died to teach, but which it rarely has the courage to remember: that men take their standing, not from what they have or what they seem, but from what they are; therefore the only ambition worthy of them is to become what they ought to be.

Hence all subsequent ages have regarded St. Dominic as one of the greatest exponents of true democracy, and his Order as one of the best examples of it. It has even been claimed for him that he was the first to embody the democratic aspirations of his age in an institution, and that through Simon de Montfort he first led England, and so the modern world, towards a system of popularly elected governments. To make such a claim is to have missed his true greatness and misread history. Experiments in democracy were begun before he interested himself in them. His first organization of a community was monarchical: he made its superior an abbot. Like St. Thomas Aquinas, he was disposed both by tradition and his native reason to prefer monarchy to any other form of government as long as he himself was not the monarch. The constitution he gave his Order is monarchical before it begins to be democratic; as its first principle of government it enunciates its absolute subjection in all things to the authority of the pope. If a democrat is a man who thinks in terms of his own rights and other men's duties, the name ought never be given to St. Dominic. What he taught his contemporaries, both conservatives and progressives, was the old Christian doctrine that slavery and serfdom can only be abolished when every man willingly becomes a slave for love of God and the brethren. Modern democracy can only claim him among its pioneers in so far as it has profited by his teaching and example of that lesson.

To the great strength of mind and will which enabled Dominic to become "powerful in word and work" nature added a most exquisite sensibility of temperament. Educated from his youth under the discipline of religion, he more and more refined these natural gifts, and became, conspicuously to his age, a living example of that perfection of nature by grace, which is one of the grand themes of St. Thomas Aquinas, and all the great Dominican theologians. His delicate sensibility was refined by the life-long practice of a spotless virginity. When he came to die this was the virtue for which he was most grateful. In his life-time its effects were noticeable in the intensity of his purified affections and in the severe asceticism with which love constrained him to rule himself. His contemporaries describe his zeal for souls as a passion, and tell us that whenever he spoke it was either to God or of God. The fervour of his prayers moved him to tears and groans, and kept him on his knees most of the night. Though most solicitous that his brethren should have all the simple comforts their health required, he himself had no bed of his own. During his vigils he scourged himself cruelly, as though the daily discipline of rigorous fasts, long journeys on foot, and much preaching were not enough to keep his flesh in training for the arduous service to which he had dedicated himself.

That his temper was not soured but sweetened by all this austerity is insisted upon by all who have recorded their impressions of him. "Athlete" became universally recognized as the *mot propre* with which to describe him, and it is so used as to imply all the finer qualities we are wont to attribute to a Greek hero and a modern sportsman. By her use of the epithet in the Bull of his canonization and many other documents of the highest authority, the Church has blessed the word and consecrated it to express the fruits of supernatural grace which she most approved in him, and which she looks for as the special characteristic of the Order that bears his name.

Religious discipline reached to every part of his nature. His mind as well as his moral character was perfected by it, and that in an age when clerical training was in danger of being discredited by the sorry results it was producing. Sacred Scripture was the instrument of Dominic's education; its principal exercise was contemplation. For him all science was embraced in the study of the Word of God; obedience to it was the most liberal and finest of all arts. His schooling lasted all his life. Until thirty-three he was a pupil, then he became a teacher as well, communicating the fruits of his contemplation to others. He did not become a master immediately; during the first years of his apostolate he served as an apprentice under his bishop, Diego. Even after that, before graduating finally, he went back to school again.

All this is reproduced in the life of his Order. The true Dominican is a life-long scholar; however old he grows he never reaches the age for leaving school, and like a school-boy he is restrained by daily discipline from mere intellectualism and all other idle pastimes. In his youth his mind is trained in unremitting study of Sacred Science—which in the Dominican vocabulary, as in the language of St. Thomas, is synonymous with Sacred Scripture. Study for him means, not browsing or random research, but a strict and formal drill: he has his daily theses to learn by heart, his dissertations to write and submit to public criticism, his debates both formal and free to conduct. Meanwhile his will is being trained by fasts and abstinences as austere as his young strength can bear, by public acknowledgment of breaches of rule, by silence, and by bells that interrupt his sleep and keep him moving briskly all day long. When at last he is licensed to preach or teach, he still remains for long years an apprentice working under supervision. He still has his appointed exercises, and examination following examination. His progress has been more than usually rapid and brilliant if by middle age he has become a Master in Sacred Theology, or a

Preacher General qualified to lead others out into the open. Even then he is still bound by the clause in his Constitutions to be "so intent on study as to be always reading or meditating something, by day and by night, at home and on the road."

IV

THE CONSTITUTION OF ST. DOMINIC

The fourth Council of the Lateran was convoked by Innocent III in April 1213 and assembled in the November of 1215. There had not been before so large a gathering of prelates in Western Christendom—a fact which proves not only the energy of the great pontiff, but also the consciousness of the clergy (even the more apathetic and worldly) that the times were critical and that all the resources of the Church were being called upon.

Fulke of Toulouse was at the Council and had taken Dominic with him. They arrived early and were received by the pope. On the eighth of October he formally approved the foundation at Prouille and took the convent under his special protection.

Of the petition which Fulke was about to address to the Council on behalf of Dominic—for recognition by the Church of himself and his companions as official preachers—we hear nothing as yet. This and subsequent events have led some historians to suppose that Dominic had ambitions to which the pope was not entirely favourable. Nothing is less in keeping with the character and aims of the two men or with the facts that are known to us. If Innocent had formally blessed Dominic's work at this point he could only have sanctioned it as a purely local institution in a single, and exceptional, diocese. Nothing is more certain than his desire that every diocese should follow the example of Toulouse. That he hesitated to create a new religious Order is beyond all question; there are facts as well as legends to prove that. But he hesitated, not because St. Dominic was pushing him too fast but because he had already gone so fast himself as to land himself in difficulties with the bishops, who had well-grounded complaints against the excesses of the converts who had been formed into religious Orders and licensed to preach.

It was precisely to meet those difficulties that he had assembled as many bishops as possible in Council. Therefore, the whole question of the preachers for whom he had long been calling was left to be dealt with at the Council—and after.

The question came up. Whoever raised it, or however it was raised, the answer sent Dominic hurrying back to Toulouse to set to work immediately on the foundation of an Order of

Preachers with a mission as wide as the Church. In its tenth canon the Council decreed: "The bishops will provide themselves with men fit to exercise, profitably to souls, the office of holy preaching; men powerful in works and in words, who, in the place of bishops unable to do so, shall when necessary visit their flocks with a zeal for their edification by word and example. The bishops will supply the needs of these preachers so that they will not be obliged through lack of anything necessary to give up their work. Hence we ordain that in cathedral and conventual churches there be appointed competent men whom the bishops may have to assist them in their work, not only in the office of preaching, but also in the hearing of confessions and all that concerns the salvation of souls." The thirteenth canon says: "For fear lest too great a diversity of religious orders create serious confusion in the Church of God, we forbid henceforth all new foundations. Whoever wishes to enter religion must choose one of the existing orders, and for the foundation of every religious house the rule and way of life of the orders already approved must be adopted."

Innocent's difficulty in reforming the state of religion had been principally with the bishops themselves. Many of them had been offended by his formation of new religious orders amongst the enthusiastic converts from heresy in Lombardy and Languedoc. It is evident that they have forced the thirteenth canon on the pope, and that he has not initiated it but accepted it as a compromise. That it could be a help, not a hindrance, to his plans for reform Dominic was very quickly to prove.

The tenth canon is likewise a concession to the bishops full of encouragement for Dominic. While leaving the reform of each diocese in the hands of its ordinary, it proposes Toulouse as an example for the whole Church, and obliges every bishop not only to employ men like Dominic, but to give them an official standing in their churches, and even, when necessary, a maintenance. By throwing on them the burden of finding such men, it ensures a welcome for those Dominic is gathering about him.

The necessity of adopting the rule and way of life of an existing order was very far from creating a problem for Dominic. The thing was already done. He himself had long professed the Rule of St. Augustine, and it was precisely by following faithfully the way of life it prescribed that he had been led to the point where he now stood. He had already given this same Rule to the nuns at Prouille. Even had he been ordered to draw up a new rule it could not conceivably have been other than an adaptation of that on which he had formed himself and others. The Rule of St. Augustine is a brief summary of the principles which must of necessity govern any Christian community of men or women living together under monastic obedience. In every age it has been found the simplest and most easily adaptable in the Church. It was especially adapted to the expansion of monastic life into the apostolic life of preachers. Unlike the Benedictine Rule it imposed no obligation of stability—that is, of permanent attachment to the convent in which profession was made. Unlike the Carthusian and Cistercian reforms it did not tie down those professing it to enclosure, or to any special duties, such as manual labour or an elaborate liturgy; but left them free, individually and corporately, for any work that might fall to them provided only that this was not inconsistent with the vows of obedience, poverty and chastity with which it is principally and very simply concerned.

St. Dominic's life with his brethren at Prouille and Toulouse shows how far he was from any thought of departing from the simple injunctions of this Rule. More significant still, perhaps, is the fact that though he followed Diego's example so faithfully in everything else, he never imitated his adoption of the Cistercian habit. It would almost seem that he himself must have encouraged Innocent to yield to the prejudice of the bishops against innovations in religious foundations.

Be that as it may, immediately after the Council he hastened back with Fulke of Toulouse, and drew up what became known later as the Book of Customs, and later still as the First Distinction of the Constitutions of the Order of Preachers. It was based on the Constitutions of the Austin Canons of Prémontré. With a few modifications, most of which were made in the life-time of St. Dominic and under his supervision, it remains to this day the religious rule of life of all Friars Preachers, severally and corporately. It is entirely disciplinary; it regulates the inner life of individuals and communities with a view to their special work of preaching the Gospel and defending the authority of the Church by all their words and in all their works. There is no mention yet of organization, legislation or government; that remained to be developed experimentally and formulated later in the Second Distinction.

The division of the Constitutions into two Distinctions continued until very recently. At the present time, by an easy process quite consistent with their own primitive provisions, the Constitutions are being revised so as to be brought into strict conformity, even in externals, with the Canon Law of the Church as revised in the Codex of 1917. This has entailed a rearrangement of parts, so that the old First Distinction now falls under two distinct headings according as it treats of Persons and of Things. But both in its old form, and as it now stands, this primitive part of the Constitutions,—excepting the Prologue which at a very early date began to differ from its Premonstratensian original in important respects,—though it bears many traces of having been adapted for the use of preachers and students, makes no explicit mention of preaching or apostolic work as the special end it has in view. It lays down the simple monastic observances by which the brethren are to regulate their own interior and domestic life, and train new recruits. The whole Divine Office is to be recited in choir, "briefly and succinctly, so that the Brethren may not lose devotion, and that their studies may be impeded as little as possible." Simple ceremonies for its decorous recital are outlined: they consist of nothing more than certain prescribed genuflections and prostrations, and the alternate sitting and standing of each side of the choir in turn. In a brief expansion of the text of the Rule of St. Augustine directions are given regulating matters of food, sleep and clothes. Though we know from other sources that dispensations in these matters were liberally allowed from the first for the sake of study and preaching, except in the Prologue there is no mention of these in the traditional text. A very strict rule of silence is enjoined. None may be received as clerics who are unable to read or ignorant of grammar. At profession all, clerics and lay-brethren, bind themselves by the three vows of poverty, chastity and obedience, Until the present revision the text still spoke of a further promise of "stability and common life". From the very outset mobility was much more characteristic of the Friars than stability. In the monastic language of the time the latter word signifies permanent attachment to the monastery in which profession was made. It applied to the first Friars Preachers in this sense, though more loosely than to the monks; because, though they were more easily movable than these, they belonged for life to the convent in which they received the habit unless they were sent elsewhere to found another, or for some good reason transferred to another already founded. But the survival of the word in this isolated instance would be surprising were it not explained by the fact that St. Dominic carefully built his Order on established traditions, not changing anything but developing everything; and by the further fact that in drawing up his original Book of Customs, from the actual text of which the word has evidently survived, his own natural disinclination for mere novelties was reinforced by the decrees of the General Council from which he was just returned.

Before ever the Council had spoken, and before Dominic and his companions had qualified to become a definite religious foundation, Fulke had given him both an official position and a conventual home in his diocese. He now took a more deliberate step towards the establishment of the preachers as a body with a recognized standing in the Church. In strict conformity with the decrees of the Council he invited his cathedral chapter to give them the chapel of St. Romain, and assisted them to build their first regular convent adjoining it. In his last official act before leaving for the Council Dominic was described as his "Minister of Preaching." Now, in the act assigning St. Romain to him and his brethren, he is called "Brother Dominic, Prior and Master of Preachers".

Having spent the greater part of 1216 in Toulouse St. Dominic returned to Rome at the end of that year. Innocent III had died in the July. On December 22nd his successor, Honorius III, approved the foundation at St. Romain as a permanent institute of regular canons. With the evident intention of conforming to the Lateran decree against new orders, the Bull of confirmation made no mention whatever of any special purpose which might seem to distinguish the new foundation from other communities of Augustinian canons already existing. That the omission was deliberate and diplomatic was made plain the very next day. On December 23rd Honorius published a second Bull so carefully worded that it cannot possibly have been an afterthought, but must have been prepared at the same time as the first. It is addressed to "his dear son Dominic and to the brethren who have made or shall make profession of the regular life," and runs, "Considering that the brethren of your Order are to be the champions of the faith and true lights of the world, we confirm your Order and take it under Our government." The phrase "True lights of the world" is consecrated in the liturgy to the Apostles and Evangelists. Diplomatically the first apostolic religious foundation is being introduced officially to the Church.

The form and language of this second Bull was unprecedented, and its consequences, as we know, changed the whole face of Christendom. But the transition as officially recognized was so imperceptible at first that even the brethren whom St. Dominic had left behind at Toulouse were apparently puzzled and even troubled by language that said so little and meant so much. Dominic, sure of his ground, had led them to expect great things; the result of his application to Rome when reported to them was no more than a commonplace approval of their way of life, with a few high-sounding words of encouragement added as a postscript. The pope himself in a letter to the brethren dated 21st January, 1217, makes it very plain how the Bull is to be understood. He insists on their mission as preachers, recognizing them as such in fact—"invincible athletes of Christ"—and urging them to pursue their apostolic vocation even if necessary to the laying down of their lives. He bids them authoritatively to "preach the divine word in season and out of season, despite every obstacle and every refusal".

St. Dominic spent the Lent in Rome, by command of the pope, preaching and lecturing in the papal palace; whence originated, it is said, the office of "Master of the Sacred Palace", always held by one of his sons. He returned to Toulouse in May, and in August assembled his brethren at Prouille. In all they numbered no more than sixteen as yet. On the Feast of the Assumption, to their astonishment and dismay, he appointed one of them abbot, split them into small parties for immediate dispersion throughout Europe, and announced his own intention of retiring to Tartary at last to preach to the heathen there.

He could not have left a clearer proof that the work he had achieved since his first attempt to go there was none of his own ambitious seeking, but rather a heavy task imposed upon him then by Innocent III. In his opinion that task was now completed; the Church now possessed, as an established fact, the corps of apostolic preachers for whom she had long been calling, and for whose official creation two popes had laboured so persistently. From this point onwards it becomes impossible to credit St. Dominic with any other ambition than is implied in simple obedience to authority and to that irresistible force of external circumstances which all good Christians recognize as the Will of God. For the rest of his career he is obviously acting on no preconceived plan, but under pressure of his own simple zeal for souls, of ecclesiastical authority, and of natural circumstances. He does not go to the East. The personage he has placed at the head of the Order remains a person of no importance. Within six months the sixteen brethren, whose sole diploma is a papal commendation for apostolic simplicity, have supplied the great international universities of Paris and Bologna with teachers whom students are soon flocking to hear and professors to join. They have a colony in Spain and a convent in Rome. They have retained Dominic to serve them as their Master. He has accepted this office and title since Christ did not refuse it, and the age allows it to those whose majesty is derived, not from rank or estates, but from their personal worth and teaching authority. The pope has written to all the bishops of Christendom bidding them welcome and support the regular preachers who are shortly coming into every diocese with an authorized mission. Within three short years Dominic has become a familiar figure in the streets of countless French, Italian and Spanish cities. In all of them he has preached to the eager intelligent audiences that are rousing Europe from its lethargy; in many of them he has gathered brilliant recruits and founded convents. As he goes on foot from town to town, he preaches by the wayside, he reads as he strides along, he entertains his companions to divine conversation, he prays, he fasts, he scourges himself, he sleeps on the hard ground, and day and night he sings aloud to heaven for very joy.

Under this kind of leadership his Order grew, numerically and organically. There were no theoretical preliminaries. The new society lived and worked in simple obedience to the laws of nature, of God, and of His Church. The natural causes that were everywhere producing constitutional government, democratic freedom, and an intellectual renaissance, here bore their happiest fruits; for expedience, reason and the authority of the Church were each unselfishly obeyed, the first in subordination to the second and the second to the third. Hence when the time came for the new society to formulate its laws, it had only to sit down and reflect upon itself; and the result at once became the recognized model for subsequent legislation, both in the Church and in secular society.

The first deliberative assembly of the Order was held on the feast of Pentecost, at Bologna, in 1220, after three years of intense life. The next sat in the same place, on the same feast, the year following. In the August of 1221 St. Dominic died. He and his brethren had already tried out experimentally and finally formulated on paper the principles by which they had lived and worked together hitherto, and were to be bound henceforth—excepting only three points: dispensations, sanctions, and corporate poverty; the first two to be settled almost immediately, the last to be the subject of experiment for several generations.

The first principle which has ruled the Order throughout its history is its dedication by the Church to the apostolic work of preaching and the salvation of souls. Immediately following on that is the law that its members must be men of prayer and ascetic life, graduating by intense and uninterrupted study to be authoritative teachers. As a society its first principle is absolute and immediate subjection, both as a clerical and monastic body, to the pope. Under his authority, it forms an independent and autonomous society; its rulers are elected by democratic suffrage; its laws are formulated by representative assemblies, and administered by officials responsible to them but enjoying full dominion and jurisdiction over their immediate subjects during their term of office.

To ascertain how these principles work out in practice there are two tests, which are strictly correlatives of one another The history of the Order at any stage of its life, and the official legislation of that period, may be consulted either together or indifferently. Each perfectly reflects the other, for the laws of the Order are the life of the Order. As they stand to-day the Constitutions are still in actual process of development; yet their continuity with the earliest Dominican legislation is complete.

The corporate aim of the Order of Preachers is still to communicate by preaching and teaching, in word and writing, the fruits which proceed by prayer and study from the overflowing fulness of contemplation. The means by which this end is pursued are the three solemn vows of the regular life and monastic observance with solemn choral recitation of the Divine Office. With the exception of the vows, these means may be modified to suit varying conditions and circumstances; but they can never be entirely dispensed with or substantially changed.

Except where exempted by the Holy See, the Order is bound by the Canon Law common to the whole Church; it is also bound by the following laws, which interpret one another in the order given: the Rule of St. Augustine; the Constitutions proper to the Order; the Ordinations of General Chapters; the Ordinations of Masters General. These are further interpreted in each Province by the Ordinations of the Provincial Chapter and the Provincial Prior; in each Priory by the Ordinations of the Conventual Prior. Constitutions are made or repealed by the vote of three successive General Chapters. Ordinations are temporary laws which cease when the Chapter or superior enacting them makes way for a successor.

Decrees of the Holy See addressed to the Order bind all its members in virtue of their vow of obedience and under pain of sin. The Rule, Constitutions and Ordinations do not bind under sin, but only under penalty; unless they are broken out of contempt, or unless it is explicitly stated that they are imposed "as a formal precept in virtue of holy obedience". A Prior cannot bind his whole community under precept without the sanction of the Provincial; nor the Provincial his whole Province without the support of his Council.

No constitution can become a dead letter. It stands until revoked by the authority and the process that makes it. Only General Chapters, or in the interval the Master General, can decide that because of circumstances it is not binding on the whole Order. At his profession each religious promises to obey the Constitutions as they stand literally, and not merely as they are held to bind at the moment. A custom, provided it is general, of long standing, and consistent with legislation, has the force of a Constitution, and can only be abolished by three successive General Chapters.

The power of dispensation in matters of religious discipline is vested in the Master General, the Provincials and the Priors, for themselves and their respective subjects. It is meant to be used, both by superiors and subjects; and is principally intended to release them from such monastic observances as may from time to time interfere with study, preaching and the good of souls.

The studies of the clerics are very carefully regulated. Every Province with sufficient resources must have a *studium generale* or major school of university standard. Such a school may grant degrees, even to outsiders, and must be staffed with a Regent, a Bachelor and a Master of Studies. The Regent is head of the house as a school. The course consists of three years of philosophy and four of theology, with as many cognate sciences as there are professors for. Where possible all lectures in Theology are doubled, a higher course being provided for those whose success in annual examinations qualifies them to prepare for degrees. To these in their last two years are granted certain exemptions from choral duties. In their studies a very rigid and formal accuracy is required of them; they must keep to the strict letter of their texts, especially the Scriptures and the *Summa* of St. Thomas, and commit as much as possible of these to memory. In all Dominican schools the Scholastic method is obligatory. The teachers are bound by oath to adhere to the teaching of St. Thomas Aquinas, and in cases where his meaning is disputed to the established traditions of the Order.

The first degree is the Lectorate of Sacred Theology, taken at the end of the seven years course. After this students with an aptitude for specialized study mustbe sent to some other College of the Order, or to a University. All others, whether graduates or not, are obliged to be lifelong students, for the profit of their own souls and of their ministry.

Seven years after the Lectorate, five at least of which must be spent in teaching and the rest in special studies, the Lector may be presented for the final examination for degrees. Having passed he requires two more years' teaching experience to qualify for the degree of Bachelor, and yet another four for that of Master.

The most characteristic part of the Dominican Constitutions is that which regulates the life of the Order as a self-governing society. The normal social unit is the Priory, under a Prior elected by the community. Priories are for the most part grouped into Provinces at the head of which are Provincial Priors elected by representatives of each Priory and of the Province as a whole. Over the whole Order, groups and individuals alike, is a Master General elected by representatives of each Province. Every superior has a Council: the Master General appoints his own; membership of Conventual and Provincial Councils is determined by seniority of rank or office. In grave matters, superiors must always consult the judgment of these bodies, and in some cases they must follow it.

Before the election of Priors and Provincials can take effect it must be confirmed by their immediate superior. The election of a Master General needs no confirmation; it becomes effective immediately, and the person elected, unless he can justify his refusal to his electors, is bound to accept office. Most other officials are not elected, but appointed by whichever of these three has authority over their office.

The powers of a Master General and of a Provincial reside *a fortiori* in General and Provincial Chapters respectively; for those officers merely execute and interpret the will of these assemblies, and are responsible for them. A General Chapter can depose a Master General; and at stated times Provincial and Conventual Chapters must vote on the efficiency and character of Provincials and Priors, and draw up a formal petition for their retention or removal. Throughout the Order the liberty of elections is very carefully safeguarded. No superior or subject may influence them by any means not guaranteed to him in the Constitutions. Superiors may not suggest candidates, except in very rare cases, when they must propose at least three; and even then subjects may choose outside these limits. All elections are by secret ballot, and conducted according to a carefully prescribed and ceremonious procedure.

A community forfeits the right to elect, and an appointment must be made by authority, if after a month's vacancy an election has not been attempted, or if after three months none has been successfully made. A Prior is elected for three years, at the end of which time he must render an account of his administration to the Provincial and to the Council of the Priory over which he has ruled. Then he retires to the place he last occupied as a subject. During his term of office he has full authority over the religious life, interior and exterior, of all in the community, and may impose upon all formal precepts binding under sin. At frequent intervals he assembles the whole community in the Chapter-house, to admonish, correct and instruct its members in all that concerns their common life. The priests publicly accuse themselves and one another of their public faults before the Prior, and receive a penance. The junior clerics and the lay-brethren make their accusations before their respective Masters. The Chapter of the house is a body with certain powers of suffrage. It consists of all the clerics who have made their final profession. Without its consent, given by secret vote, no new member can be given the habit or admitted to first Profession.

Provincials are elected for a term of four years by the Provincial Chapter. This body includes certain members of the Province privileged by reason of honourable service, all the Conventual Priors, and a representative elected from and by the subjects of each convent or other group in the Province. Before Priors can vote they must produce certificates from their communities to show that they have maintained regular observance and choral office in their convents, and supplied the principal spiritual and temporal needs of their subjects. A Provincial who has just completed two successive terms in the same Province may not regularly be re-elected in it immediately. All elections are confirmed or vetoed at will by the Master General, who must himself appoint a Provincial after seven useless scrutinies or a year's vacancy.

The Provincial Council consists of at least six members including the Masters in Sacred Theology and ex-Provincials of the Province. They hold office for life and cannot resign without permission of the Master General, or be absent without the Provincial's leave when summoned to a meeting. In their own convent, if they are subjects, they are as much under the authority of their Prior as the other Brethren. Their vote binds the Provincial in serious matters, such as new buildings or the appointment and removal of Priors. Between Provincial Chapters the Provincial requires their sanction for the settlement of any pressing business that normally belongs to the Chapter.

The Provincial Chapter meets normally every four years, and sits for eight, or at most, ten days. It elects the next Provincial, and makes Ordinations for him and the rest of the Province. Three months' notice having been given, the Provincial with his Council prepare the *agenda* and each unit in the Province elects its representative to accompany a Prior. In every Priory, the Prior and his Council draw up a statement of accounts, and those qualified to vote for a Prior secretly petition the retention or removal of their present Prior.

Two days before the election all assemble at the place appointed for the Chapter, and the Provincial, having appointed three of his Council to examine the credentials of all the voters, retires from Office at midnight. He is immediately succeeded, as Head of the Province and President of the Chapter, by the Prior of the Convent in which the Chapter is assembled. The next day all the voters elect a Committee of four, called Diffinitors, in whom the supreme legislative power of the Chapter is vested. The following day when the same voters have completed the election of a Provincial, yesterday's President gives place to the Provincial-elect, under whose presidency the authority of the Diffinitors begins immediately. This extends over the whole Province, including the Provincial, and all are bound by it under obedience. The Diffinitors alone make the Ordinations, and address admonitions to the Provincial and others. With the Provincial Council they can address petitions to the Master General, though these must not be on behalf of themselves or the Provincial-elect. At the end of the Chapter all the voters elect representatives for the next two General Chapters. The Acts of the Chapter, after examination, and, if necessary, correction, by the Master General, are promulgated throughout the Province. They stand till the next Provincial Chapter. The Provincial can only interpret them, or grant dispensations in particular cases; he cannot repeal or annul anything, nor can the Diffinitors themselves while still in authority empower him to do so. After two years of his term have elapsed, he must summon the Priors of the Province to the next meeting of the Provincial Council, where, in his absence, all must petition for his retention or removal.

The Master General is elected for twelve years by a General Chapter consisting of the ex-Masters General, the Council of the late Master General, the Provincials, and two elected representatives from each Province. The late Master General presides at the election, which must be completed on the first day of the Chapter, and for which a simple majority of votes suffices.

Following its election of a Master General, the General Chapter assembles at intervals of three years, its composition varying each time. At an elective Chapter legislative power lies with the Master General, the Provincials of the Order, and the elected representatives of each Province, all voting on equal terms. At the next assembly the Provincials are absent, and legislation rests with the Master General and the elected representatives of Provinces. These last are absent from the next gathering, the Provincials this time sitting with the Master General. The next consists again of the Master General and the elected representatives of Provinces. The series begins anew with each election of a Master General. Thus, in the legislation of the Order, subjects have a preponderating power, through their elected representatives. In this sense the Order is democratic. It is democratic also in the sense that superiors are all elected by their subjects. But in its administration and executive the Order is a constitutional monarchy. Every subject is bound by obedience to execute, instantly and without question, the lawful commands and judgments of his superior. At any given moment the power of the latter to interpret and enforce the law is limited only by his own superiors, and a Council that is not elected. Subject only to the Constitutions and standing Ordinations, the authority of the Master General is absolute; the members of his Council are appointed and dismissed by himself at will. To maintain a perfect balance between the democratic and monarchical forces in the Order, the Constitutions very solemnly forbid, under the severest penalties, any attempt by Provincials on the one hand, and elected representatives on the other, to aim legislation of any kind against one another.

As they stand to-day the laws of monastic observance are substantially unchanged from the form in which St. Dominic left them. Such modifications as there are have been introduced either under pressure of Canon Law, or as a recognition that secular civilization has progressed in a few minor and material respects. Thus, the suppression of the law of periodical bloodletting is an acknowledgment of the advance of the science and art of medicine. The influence of later religious orders backed sometimes by Canon Law has also made itself felt.

From the earliest times the Constitutions have regulated the work of preaching by careful but simple rules. They have never discussed this principle work of the Order in terms of mere oratory. They understand it to mean always the communication to others by word and example of the fruits of monastic contemplation. It is significant that the Order of Preachers, so formal in everything else, has no elaborate technique or pulpit oratory. For its preaching is not merely an art, but a life including all the arts. That it has achieved high perfection in them all is one of the commonplaces of history. But apart from a certain elementary training in what throughout the Church is now called "sacred eloquence", the Constitutions make as little provision for the training of pulpit orators as for that of poets, painters, sculptors, architects and the rest. "Preaching by word and example" is left undefined so as to limit the range of the Order's activities as little as possible. In prayer, in monastic discipline, in its social life, in study even, the Order makes very definite and very detailed regulations for its members; but preaching, the end to which these things are means, is not only itself undefined and unspecified in detail, it overrules definitions and details elsewhere. All the emphasis of the Constitutions is thrown into one sentence. "Preach, by word and example"; which is equivalent to saying: "Preach, anyhow, but *preach!*" That emphasis explains the note of liberty throughout all Dominican law and life. The Friar is exempt from all laws except those which preaching requires: he may preach any way he chooses, like St. Thomas, St. Antoninus, James of Voragine, Fra Angelico, Volmar of Colmar, Lacordaire. There is only one restraint on his liberty; he can do or be what he likes, but he *must* preach, by word and example. He must make his whole life a sermon, and the best sermon for which God has given him talent and grace. The liberty of Christianity leaves a man free to do good, and only forbids him what is evil. That it forbids under sin. The liberty of the Order of Preachers leaves a Friar free to do his best, and only forbids him to do less than his best. That it forbids under penalty, not under sin. It is therefore a rule of perfection; that is to say, a religious rule. It only differs from other religious rules by being what Dominicans, following Aristotle and Cicero, call more "formal".

V

THE CHARACTER OF THE ORDER OF PREACHERS

The contemplative life was the vocation which St. Dominic first chose for himself. He dedicated himself to the cloister by an irrevocable vow. In the Catholic Church the cloister is a traditional institution and a very venerable one. It has always stood for retirement from the world and contemplation. With regard to this tradition St. Dominic was, as usual, staunchly conservative before he was progressive. He remained a contemplative all his life. When in response to the needs of his age he came out of his cloister into the world, he was not taking a step backwards or undoing anything already done. He was merely enlarging his cloister by making it as wide as the world, and increasing the community of contemplatives to which he already belonged. He continued to speak exclusively to God or of God. After the Epistles of St. Paul his favourite reading was the Conferences of Cassian; wherever he went he carried with him a copy of this "mirror for monks" as St. Benedict called the book. He preached by word and example; the example being that of a contemplative at large, the words being those of a contemplative praying aloud. His first foundation was a convent of contemplative nuns. He made his brethren preachers by making them contemplatives first. They, too, were to preach by word and example; the manner of their preaching was to be contemplative, its matter contemplated. The older contemplative Orders provided the safeguards of a cloister for those who had decided to become contemplatives before entering it. The Order of Preachers came into existence to propagate contemplation: *contemplata aliis tradere.* In his treatise on "Truth"—the motto of his Order—St. Thomas shows this to mean, not that the contemplative gives his conclusions to others, to be received by them on faith or as opinions, but that he assists them to form in themselves minds like his own, and more and more independent of his as his work for them goes on.

Hence Dominican work for souls is educational in the highest sense, as distinct from merely pastoral. It aims rather to educate consciences, and rather to train men and women to think and act for themselves, than to guide, protect and correct them by particular directions. It is the tendency of this Order, more even than of the Franciscan Order which has so much in common with it, to draw intimately into its own life all with whom it comes in contact, making them Dominican contemplatives: that is to say, contemplatives active in the spread of contemplation, and independent when necessary of monastic enclosure. The lay-brothers of the First Order, the cloistered nuns of the Second, and the men and women, conventual and secular, of the Third are all truly Dominicans. They are leagued as one family to propagate the contemplation of Truth, winning others by example always, by word of mouth whenever there is call for this.

An eminent modern historian of the Order,* speaking of the causes of religious disorder in the fourteenth century, has said: "The Order of Preachers, which should have remained a select body, developed beyond bounds and absorbed some elements unfitted to its form of life." A purely contemplative order must obviously increase its numbers with caution. There is no less, and perhaps even more, need for caution in the case of an Order whose vocation is contemplation in action. Clearly defined limits are imposed upon the Dominican

* P. Mandonnet, O.P. In the *Catholic Encyclopædia*, vol. xii, p. 358 s.v. Preachers.

Order both in the scope of its activity and the extent of its membership; and this by reason of something which might be considered a limitation in St. Dominic himself, were it not that the same trait appears in the Master upon whose example he so carefully modelled himself. Jesus Christ declared that He was come to call, not just men, but sinners to repentance. Nevertheless, with two outstanding exceptions, He treated the sinners with as much respect as if they were all just men of the highest character and intelligence. The Pharisees and the traders in the temple were the exceptions. They alone were denounced and scourged : the money-changers because they made the house of God a den of thieves, the hypocritical Pharisees because they had taken away the key of knowledge, neither entering in themselves nor allowing others to enter. The Order of Preachers has earned itself many hard names for its fierce denunciation of two classes of men : simoniacal prelates and propagators of error. St. Thomas Aquinas, always so respectful towards the Papacy, used his strongest language to denounce simony there; and St. Catherine of Siena follows his example. To recall the attitude of the Order to those who disseminate error it is enough to mention the mere name of the Inquisition. In everybody else St. Dominic and his Order have always assumed good faith and good will. The only weapon they have employed against individual heretics and sinners has been the painstaking exposition of Truth. It was from the first the assumption of St. Dominic that, their leaders excepted, the Albigensians were sound at heart and confused in mind. He took it for granted that to introduce them to Truth was to lead them directly to all virtue. His limitation, if such it may fairly be called, was an apparent inability to conceive malice or meanness in another. The same characteristic is very deeply ingrained in his Order. It has a very strict penal code providing against every kind of delinquency amongst its members; but this code expressly excludes the assumption of malice in the delinquent. Hence that Dominican insistence on the liberty of the individual and his right to be trusted which must often appear excessive to those whose vocation is more expressly to "rebuke the unquiet, comfort the feeble-minded and support the weak." The same critics also find that Dominicans have an exaggerated respect for the intelligence of simple people, are too prone to see good in sinners and truth in heresy, are too impatient of easy explanations of doctrine and labour-saving refutations of error, too ready to concede points to an unscrupulous or prejudiced opponent, and too apt in their zeal for Truth to scandalize weaker brethren and offend pious ears.

That his vocation undoubtedly exposes him to these dangers every Dominican is obliged to admit; and there are few who have not, from time to time, had reason to be thankful for wholesome reminders that theirs is not the only Order in the Church, but one of many raised up to help each other, as much by rivalry as by co-operation, under the pastoral care of an authority higher than them all. But since rivalry implies something resembling opposition, and since the Dominican Order has nothing to oppose to anybody but the truth and its high commission to teach this, the Dominican in controversy inevitably takes up the attitude of being the rightful teacher of all who oppose him, bowing to none but the highest authority in the Church. He will hear of no compromise on grounds of expedience, prudence or even charity, insisting that to satisfy without mitigation the strictest claims of Truth, whether Scriptural, traditional, metaphysical or logical, is the only sure way to satisfy every other claim that can legitimately be urged.

The history of the Dominican Order has two sides; first a continuous record of constructive work gratefully admired and assimilated throughout the Church; second an equally continuous record of theological controversies within the Church. These controversies are inevitable whenever the Order is worthily fulfilling its mission, and properly understood they redound to the credit of all concerned in them. By far the keenest of them have arisen between the Order of Preachers and the two religious bodies to whom it stands nearest in many important ways, and with whom it has exchanged many very precious gifts: the Order of Friars Minor and the Society of Jesus.

The root of their differences lies deep in history. The Order of Preachers first came into being to combat the Albigensian heresy. Most other heresies, and all later ones, including those of Hus, Wicklif, Luther and the rest, began within the Church and at first claimed Scriptural authority for their doctrines. The Albigensian doctrines originated outside the Church and were more opposed to Christian Doctrine than any which engaged any of the Fathers, excepting St. Augustine. Following the Manichees whom he refuted, the Albigenses were in error on the deep metaphysical questions of the universal causality of God and the nature and origin of evil. But the Albigenses had long been neighbours of Christian peoples. Like the Jews and Mahommedans who had influenced them they were well acquainted with the Christian Scriptures, and welcomed their support whenever reason was able to interpret them favourable to their own doctrines. They had also felt, unmoved, the pressure of those arguments against the Manichees by which St. Augustine had enriched Catholic thought. The first task, therefore, which fell to the Dominican Order was to appeal to reason to support the full Catholic traditional interpretation of Scripture, and to urge the profound reasoning of St. Augustine with still fuller reasoning. In a very short time this led the Order to the position defined by St. Thomas at the beginning of his *Summa*. Theology, he explains, is a science which argues from the truths revealed in Scripture and accepted without any proof but the authority of God. It uses human reason, not to prove what is believed, but to make clear other things which are put forward in theology. For as grace does not destroy nature but makes it perfect, reason must be of service to faith. Therefore, theology makes use even of the authority of the philosophers wherever they were able to know the truth by reason. But theology uses such authorities only as extraneous and probable arguments. It uses the authority of Scripture as its proper and conclusive arguments; the authority of the other Doctors of the Church as its proper, but only probable, arguments. For our faith rests on the revelation made to

Apostles and Prophets, not on the revelation (if any) made to other Doctors. And he concludes by quoting St. Augustine: "Only those books of Scripture which are called canonical have I so learned to fear and honour that I firmly believe none of their authors to have erred in writing anything. Others I so read that, however they may excel in holiness and learning, I do not for that reason think their opinions to be true."

The first great controversy in which the Dominican Order was concerned arose when it was found that St. Thomas and his master Blessed Albert the Great were taking St. Augustine at his word; that is, not accepting his teaching on faith, but checking it on all points of natural philosophy by the teaching of Aristotle, and even elucidating it with their own reasoning. Thus their very logical conservatism in the tradition of St. Augustine at once led them to be opposed as departing from his doctrine. At first many of their own brethren, whose early education was outside the Order, joined in this opposition; but St. Thomas was soon recognized to be the genuine Dominican; the whole Order grew to be of one mind with him. Strong opposition was, however, maintained by the Franciscans, with St. Bonaventure as their leader. But the difference between the two schools and the two saints at the head of each, is no more than the difference between St. Dominic and St. Francis. The difference is often explained by reference to the mysticism and poetry of the Franciscans and the stern intellectualism of the Dominicans. But this will not do. Stern intellectualism is not opposed to poetry and mysticism. In this case both occur together on each side; St. Thomas was a rare poet and mystic, and St. Bonaventure a very good philosopher. The difference and its reconciliation must be sought in the diverse yet complementary nature of the two Orders. The Friars Preachers were founded to win to Christ the minds of men whose wills were good; the Friars Minor to win to Christ the hearts of men whose morals were relaxed but whose minds were as well informed on Catholic doctrine as was that of St. Francis himself. If St. Dominic had a defect it would seem to have been inability to conceive of a man whose heart was evil or of one whose mind was not full of questions for Christ to answer. If St. Francis had a defect it must have been inability to see how anything but moral fault could keep a man from joyously accepting anything and everything that Christ and His Church might choose to teach. St. Dominic's mission was to fill men's minds as full of truth as they could hold; the mission of St. Francis was to fill men's hearts as full of love as they could hold. From the first it was evident that though the emphasis was different the two were doing the same work. As their Orders developed the difference was further emphasized, yet at the same time the resemblance became more marked. St. Thomas sang and prayed to the piping of St. Francis, but with emphasis on the part played by the mind in both song and prayer; St. Bonaventure philosophized as sedately as any Dominican, but was all the time emphatically a philosopher with a heart. St. Thomas speaks of bliss as the knowledge of God. Truth is his aim; pursue that, he implies, and you will rejoice in Beauty and love Goodness. For St. Bonaventure bliss is the love of God. Truth is not for him so much an end as a means, and an austere means, to love. There must be, he insists, a constant effort of the will to turn the mind to God, and so to arrive at more perfect love of Him. Those who followed St. Bonaventure ended by asserting the superiority of the will over the intellect. St. Thomas and his followers teach that but for the intellect the will would be a mere brute appetite; the highest perfection of men and angels is the intellectual activity by which God is seen in the Beatific Vision. It was left for the genius of Dante to show that the difference, though real, is in effect no difference.

Dominican theology and philosophy very

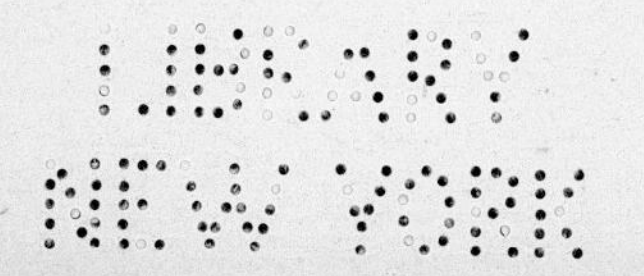

rapidly attained their perfection at the hands of St. Thomas. After that, like the Order itself, they both progressed in very many directions, but always conservatively on foundations which were never changed. This was not because the Order lacked great thinkers, or because Dominican minds were stereotyped; but because each generation became as intellectually satisfied with the work of its predecessors as St Dominic was satisfied with the traditions on which he built. With the Franciscans it was otherwise. Even their philosophy retained the playful spirit of St. Francis which loved to disport itself in the exuberant variety of nature, making every flower the starting point of a new ascent to heaven. They produced a galaxy of original and inventive geniuses, most of whom flourished in England, where variety has always been favoured. Many of them luxuriated in the mathematical and physical sciences, which are as rich in opportunities for the play of fancy as the game of chess. Scotus, the greatest of them all, played subtly round the solid work of St. Thomas, and so brilliantly expressed the inventive Franciscan genius, that for a time all his brethren seemed tempted to surrender their originality to his. That could not be, however. Even in evil days, others, like William of Occam, struck out new lines, and kept the conservative Domi-

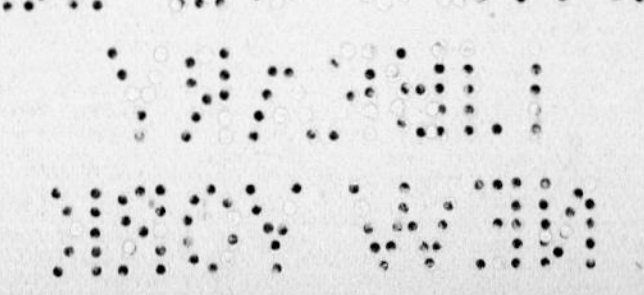

nican steadily employed in such development of their tradition as was necessary to deal with his sallies. Thus, in matters of doctrine the Dominican School stands opposed to the Franciscan as the more conservative to the more liberal. Accordingly, on the question of the Immaculate Conception, while the Franciscans pressed enthusiastically for a development of the doctrine, the Dominicans insisted cautiously that nothing already certain and settled should be forgotten. When eventually the Church defined the doctrine she carefully safeguarded both positions.

The world to which Dominicans and Franciscans came was simply divided into Christendom and heathendom. Within Christendom the authority of the Papacy was unquestioned. Beyond, the authority of reason could always be presumed. This state of things was very congenial to Dominicans. Their function was very like that of the ministers of education and justice in a society where peace and order prevail. Their work was constructive: the building up of Christian thought, and so morality, on foundations of faith, or at least of reason. Their attitude to Christian and pagan alike was friendly. Just as the policeman and the judge at first sight presume a man to be a good citizen, and only proceed against him as an enemy when there is evidence of guilt, so the Dominican presumed Christians to be faithful and pagans to be reasonable, unless there was plain evidence to the contrary. In the courts of the Inquisition it usually fell to them to sift such evidence. With the Reformation came a change. Within Christendom the authority of the Pope began to be openly disputed, and that in the name of reason, Scripture, tradition and everything else that was sacred to Dominicans. It was not possible to answer reason with reason, for to Dominicans reasoning meant the scholastic tradition of their Order, and by the Reformers this was as much despised as the authority of the Pope.

In secular society when sedition breaks out and authority and traditional ways of thinking are openly called into question, the laws of nature require that the freedom even of well-disposed citizens shall be restricted. Good faith is no longer presumed until the contrary is proved; good faith has rather to be proved before it can be presumed. Courts of justice become courts martial where the accused is presumed guilty unless he can prove his innocence. The friendly policeman is withdrawn from the streets, and his place is taken by the sentry and military pickets whose business it is to suspect everybody, and demand proofs of good faith before allowing anyone, friend or foe, to pass. Vigilance is keenest where there is greatest show of friendship, for friendship is the likeliest disguise of a spying and plotting enemy. Every instance of bad faith breeds distrust amongst the very people who are most trustworthy. Such a condition of things naturally calls for a dictator, a man to whom the whole might of the state is committed because he is acknowledged without question to be always right. His business is to command, not to discuss; to save the commonwealth, not to develop it. He must reserve all initiative to himself, and therefore insist on military obedience to practical orders, discouraging speculative doubts and questions and independent sallies in pursuit of the highest and best. To save what is vital he must often sacrifice what has been built up by the long and patient labour of politicians, lawyers and teachers; and he and they will both be more than human if they do not oftentimes tax each other's patience sorely, and even question each other's loyalty to the best interests of the state.

Nature, says St. Thomas, is not destroyed but perfected by grace. Christ's "New Law" of charity only intensifies the natural laws of society in the Catholic Church. The Reformation brought into action, as nothing before had done, the dictatorial powers of the Papacy. As a result of this the Order of Preachers practically went out of employment as a world-force for the duration of Protestantism.

The first reaction of the Church to Protestantism was the Council of Trent. A great part of its work was reconstruction and development on old foundations, and in this the leading part fell to Dominicans. Their success was so great that one of their number, St Pius V, the only canonized Pope since the Reformation, was elected to administer the laws of Trent. Personally he was one of the Dominicans in whom St. Dominic has most conspicuously lived again. Yet with the exception of certain privileges accorded to his own and older Orders, the acts of his pontificate are directly opposed to the Dominican tradition which presumes good will everywhere, and encourages variety, individual liberty, speculation and initiative. The severe discipline of obedience, uniformity and vigilance over friend and foe, which is usually said to have been introduced into the Church by the Society of Jesus, began as a matter of fact with him; and the Jesuits themselves had most to suffer from it. He imposed choral duties upon them, and in other ways deprived their institute of its distinctive character. He insisted on uniformity in liturgy, prescribing the Roman Breviary and Missal for all countries; he increased the severity of penitential discipline, and reserved powers of absolution to the Papacy with unprecedented strictness; he re-established the Inquisition, giving it now the character of a court martial; he presumed bad faith in Elizabeth while there might still have been some excuse for trusting her, and thus sorely tried the loyalty of his faithful English subjects. It was while he was engaged in this restrictive legislation that his religious brethren in Spain were defending the right of St. Teresa to pray herself and others into heaven in her own characteristic way.

With kind words about his piety and the success of his prayers against the Turks, historians commonly dismiss St. Pius V as an unsuccessful ruler. Such a verdict should not pass without a protest, but it is a mere matter of words whether we call it success or failure to have demonstrated, as he did, that a new policy of stern discipline had become necessary in the Church, and that it was both unsuitable and uncongenial to the Dominican character. His successor was profiting by this lesson when he established the Society of Jesus in the Gregorian University as the teachers of philosophy and theology which the age required.

Remembering that both were saints and therefore excelled in all the virtues, it is safe to examine the difference between St. Dominic and St. Ignatius in order to understand the fundamental difference between the Dominican and Jesuit vocation. It is obviously the distinction between the constructive worker in peace-time and the defensive worker in war-time. St. Dominic beginning as a contemplative in sheltered surroundings looks to the good in men and overcomes evil by developing that good. The will, he argues, naturally seeks goodness, the mind naturally seeks truth. He therefore works on the natural goodness of the will and the natural reasonableness of the mind, proposing to each the example and teaching of Christ which can alone perfectly satisfy them. He assumes good dispositions in nature, and encourages them. It is because these good dispositions are a fact in his own case that he assumes them to be a fact in the case of others, too. When the assumption of fact is correct, and only then, he succeeds in practice. As a philosopher he is always successful, for as such it is his business to deal with the nature of things as seen from eternity. From that point of view all things are good, and evil cancels out.

St. Ignatius beginning as a soldier and man of the world, looks at facts rather than at the nature of things. His own first start has been a false one. He did not begin, like St. Dominic and St. Thomas, by patiently applying his mind to the quest of the full supernatural truth and goodness that would most perfectly satisfy even his nature. His will, anticipating and starving his mind, seizes blindly upon things which are only apparently good, and which ultimately fail him. His first salutary discovery, therefore, is not, like St. Dominic's, objective—the truth and goodness of Christ's words and example; but like that of St. Francis, subjective—the blind indifference of his own will to good and evil. Hence at the outset of their philosophy and their prayer, both Franciscans and Jesuits are less contemplative, because more self-conscious, than Dominicans; they have to reverse the order of St. Thomas, treating of moral truth before they come to speculative truth, and making purgation the way to illumination instead of regarding truth, like St. Catherine of Siena, as at once a great light and a cleansing fire. The Jesuit emphasis, like the Franciscan, is all on the will: its perilous power of blindly choosing evil, and of darkening the mind and quenching its natural thirst for truth; its need of moral reform as a step to the liberation of the mind. The Dominican mission is to men whose will is actually so good as to be urging their minds to seek truth. The mission of Franciscans and Jesuits is to men whose wills are potentially good but actually enslaved by evil, which in its turn enslaves the mind. They first of all address themselves, not like Dominicans to the mind with pure cold reason, but to the will: Jesuits directly by commands, exhortations, and threats; Franciscans, indirectly through imagination and emotion by bright fancy and the cheerful warmth of affection. This last difference brings the Franciscan nearer to the Dominican than to the Jesuit vocation : its method is more objective. At the same time it brings the Jesuit vocation nearer to the Dominican than to the Franciscan: for Jesuits and Dominicans are both more concerned with heresy and therefore with arguments in defence of faith. The moment St. Francis realized the vanity of earthly things and withdrew his will from them, nothing remained for him but to pursue the truth gaily and simply: for, excepting moral laxity, Catholic truth had no serious rival in his Umbria. Both St. Dominic and St. Ignatius found Catholic truth attacked by rivals claiming to be better truth. But the two men were different, and the situation for each was different. In St. Dominic's day it was first the reasonableness and so the authority of Catholic teaching that was challenged: hence the appeal to reason sufficed for him. In St. Ignatius' day it was first the authority, that is the moral goodness, of the Catholic Church that was resisted, hence he has to defend right rather than truth. By his contemplative training St. Dominic found his mind fully equipped to defend the reasonableness of the faith. By his military training St. Ignatius was not at first prepared to think aloud and explain. His schooling was yet to begin. Before it could profit him he had to make a *choice*—a word much more frequent in the Jesuit than the Dominican vocabulary. He found himself a soldier on a battlefield with two rival standards claiming his allegiance. His heart rather than his head told him to which side he rightfully belonged; it also reproached him with having been doubtfully loyal hitherto. Once it had spoken, he could not sit down, a philosophical spectator, and thrash out intellectually the merits of either side. The cause he loved was in danger, and needed the loyal service of men of action. He therefore bound himself and his Company to the Holy See by an explicit oath of obedience such as Dominicans, the staunchest of papal supporters before his day, had never dreamed of and could scarcely understand. For them loyalty to the Popes was the breath of life and almost a postulate of reason: it could scarcely be called deliberate. For him it was very emphatically a deliberate choice and an act of faith. As it was the mission of Dominicans to insist on the reasonableness of authority, and the rights of reason; so it became the mission of Jesuits to insist on the rights of authority and the reasonableness of rights. Hence St. Thomas is the philosopher who explains the reasonableness of faith and considers mind and will as they are by nature, free only to submit to truth and goodness; while Suarez is the philosopher who explains the reasonableness of law, and considers the will as free in fact to obey or disobey it. Crudely, though not inexcusably, Dominicans are often described as intellectualists, Jesuits as pragmatists.

In his day, like St. Dominic, St. Ignatius was the very man the Church was looking for. In the thirteenth century she was securely in being, but sorely needed St. Dominic to promote her well-being. In the sixteenth century her very existence was threatened, and she needed a soldier saint to save her from perishing. Difficulties between her old builders and her new soldiers were only naturally to be expected. In countries stricken by the Reformation the difficulties solved themselves. The Dominican Order practically died out for want of cloisters, books, philosophic calm, and an impartial leisured audience. Vocations all went to the Jesuits, as the best young men all go to the army when society is in danger. The Jesuits were naturally and rightfully given the first place in the Church, and like the military in war time, exercised especial vigilance over Dominicans who wished to philosophize and question, and over Franciscans who wanted to sing, even while Rome was burning. Real difficulties, however, arose in France, and still more in Spain, where the Reformation produced least effect. St. Dominic and St. Ignatius were both Spaniards, and all Spaniards except saints are prone to fierce partisan pride. There are always difficulties in that land between the military and the philosophers, and the land has always been rich in both. In the great quarrel that arose it is not surprising to find the Jesuits complaining that the Dominicans had no regard for the freedom of the human will, the Dominicans that the Jesuits were relapsing into old heresies which put limits to the universal causality of God. The edifying part of the spectacle is the attitude of both to papal authority: their intense rivalry turns out to be no more than a sign of intense life and a proof of intense loyalty.

The philosophy characteristic of the Dominican Order is reduced to practice in its prayer. The two great philosophical principles for which it has always stood are the universal causality of God and the unity of body and soul as a single substance in human nature. Its tradition of prayer is based on the understanding that everything in creation comes from God, belongs to Him, and must return to Him; and that it is the privilege of human nature, which not only has the use of all material natures, but gathers up all created natures in itself, to refer them all back to Him.

Prayer in its widest meaning is the whole life of an intelligent creature directed to God as its last End. According to St. Thomas that End is attained by man when his mind contemplates the divine essence in the Beatific Vision, and his heart, by consequence, finds rest there forever. Man, however, attains his end, not immediately, but through means. When, therefore, he speaks of the necessity of putting first things first, he must use a careful distinction. The first thing he intends must be the last thing he does. When he aims at the union of his mind with God, his first steps must begin in the body and in the material world. His first acts must be the exercise of the lowest faculties in his nature, and from the lowest he must rise step by step to the highest. Before he can contemplate he must reason; before he can reason he must become proficient in the use of language and of fancy; prior to this he must have developed his animal senses, including memory, instinct, and such imagination as enables even a dog to dream; and before this is possible he must have developed those powers which he possesses in common with stocks and stones. Throughout his life in this world his highest operations remain dependent on the lowest. Thus, though he may for a moment now and again attain to ecstatic states of purely spiritual understanding and love, he can never remain there long; unless he is to pass out of the body altogether—a separation he cannot naturally desire, but only accept as a painful necessity—he must again return to support his spiritual life on such vegetative and animal operations as the use of food and air, of sleep and of sense perceptions and imagery, rising again and again from these into the spiritual world by processes of discursive reason.

The whole of Dominican life is a prayer in this sense. Everything material in it—words, actions, external works, external equipment—is very formally impressed with the stamp of the spirit, and especially the stamp of mind, the highest spiritual faculty. And everything, mind especially, is centred upon God.

Both on the subjective side, in its exercises, and on the objective side, in the objects of its devotion, Dominican prayer is an orderly and natural progress from the material to the spiritual world. The liturgy of the Order is full of brisk bodily movement, including an elaborate ritual of inclinations, genuflections and prostrations, with frequent ceremonial processions from place to place. Its tradition of vocal prayer is very distinctive; words are so to be recited and sung that their character as a bodily exercise will not become lost in meditation and emotion, as is the deliberate tendency of the older monastic chant. Study, again, is a step towards contemplative prayer, very distinct in itself and very formally articulated.

Both Dominican and Franciscan traditions have made the fullest possible use of material aids to prayer for the assistance both of sense and imagination. Whereas the Franciscan genius has as usual been exuberantly inventive, often going like St. Francis to nature for its material and its inspiration, the Dominican tradition has been more conservative and restrained, holding for the most part to such time-honoured human and Christian institutions as holy water, beads and books—especially books. In its use of all such things it has stamped upon them very clearly its characteristic mark of mind informing matter.

Objectively, though Dominican prayer seeks God in His essence, this is its ultimate, not its immediate, aim. Before He can be thus attained He must first be sought in the sacred Humanity to which He has condescended for our sakes, and especially in the Blessed Eucharist which is the lowest abasement of that Humanity. The Blessed Eucharist is the living centre of the Christian religion, where it is possible for man—even before his life has advanced beyond its most elementary stage, to which belongs nourishment attained through the sense of touch alone—to become really united with God. Everything else in the Christian religion exists to lead men to the Blessed Eucharist: the other sacraments, the teaching of the Church, and all that sensible, imaginative and rational setting in which both have been enshrined by the industrious piety of generations of saints.

Thus all Dominican prayer is directed first and foremost to *Corpus Christi*, the Body and Blood of Christ. This is the great characteristic which distinguishes Dominican liturgy, Dominican mysticism, Dominican art, Dominican theology. The gathering of everything round the Blessed Sacrament is not now so conspicuously distinctive of the Order of Preachers as it was in the early days of its history, for the whole Church has long been enriched by the devotion that marked out St. Dominic, St. Thomas and St. Catherine of Siena even amongst the saints of their day. Their singular devotion to Mary the Mother of Christ was more homely than the mystical raptures of St. Bernard, and than the romantic chivalry of St. Francis, precisely because it was paid to her with especial reference to the fruit of her womb. She was the Mother who bore the Body of Christ, nursed it, trained it to manhood, and consented to its mutilation on Calvary in order that she and all others might obtain eternal life by receiving it as their food. St. Catherine's favourite devotions were to the Precious Blood, the Heart of Christ, the Holy Eucharist. St. Thomas finds all the teaching of the Church uttered by the Crucifix, for which he demands a worship such as could not be given to any other image. The Order has always had a very special devotion to St. Mary Magdalen, the sinner who by a touch of Our Lord's Flesh was made one of the greatest contemplative saints.

The moment Dominican prayer rises above the level of sense and imagination its immediate object is the inspired Word of God studied directly and intellectually in the Scriptures. A Dominican library is no more than a vast commentary on the sentences of Scripture, and all that Dominican learning aims at is a synthesis or a *Summa* of human knowledge in its relation to God as He is there revealed incarnate.

The best example of the prayer of the Order in a popular form is the Rosary. There has been much controversy in recent times about the Dominican authorship of this devotion. There is a tradition in the Church, often endorsed by Popes since the sixteenth century, that Our Lady appeared in vision to St.

Dominic and bade him recite and propagate the Rosary in the form in which we know it now. It is neither reasonable nor desirable to accept this as a literal statement of historic fact. From very early days the Order has had a zeal for the chronicling of such legends, and in 1256 it made an official collection of all bearing on its own history. Though this is avowedly incomplete, the absence of all mention of the Rosary in it and all other documents until the fifteenth century is sufficient evidence that this devotion was a late development. But that it developed within the Order in a characteristically Dominican manner, and out of elements existing there from the beginning, is beyond the possibility of a reasonable doubt. It is a prayer beginning at the finger tips. The beads which it uses as counters are a human institution as old and as widespread as mankind. Its repetition of "Our Father" and "Hail Mary," like a child's nursery rhyme, is an application of the principle that, in the early stages of human education, and indeed in all subsequent stages, sound forms of words must be repeated and memorized before their meaning can be understood: a principle strongly insisted upon in Dominican liturgy and scholastic discipline, and frequently expounded by St. Thomas in his explanations of the highest intellectual processes. With Dominicans the

Rosary like the Divine Office is regarded primarily as a choral rather than a private and silent devotion, to be recited by alternate choirs, or sung processionally with much bodily movement. This is obviously what it was originally designed to be, and in the thirteenth century Dominican version of the *Ancren Riwle* there are already signs of its development in this direction. A Dominican recommends a community of nuns to recite aloud, with a rich variety of inclinations and prostrations, a psalter of *Aves*—an institution already established in monastic life before the days of St. Dominic.

On the bodily side the Rosary has all the special characteristics of Dominican prayer. They are even more marked on the mental side. The object of the devotion is, as our English formula has it, to "contemplate" the "mysteries" of our Redemption. This is done by stimulating, through words and actions, first the imagination and then the discursive reason to entertain themselves with the Body of Christ as seen through His Mother's eyes. The Joyful Mysteries represent the oldest form of the devotion, originally known as Our Lady's Joys. Their subject matter is purely Scriptural, the incidents of Our Lord's early life, which St. Luke recorded from the lips of Mary herself, and of which he says in conclusion: "And His mother kept all these words in her heart." When it preaches the Rosary to the faithful and encourages them by its example to practise it, the Order of Preachers is fulfilling its mission with very admirable skill; by inviting them to make fanciful play around this Scriptural history, to imagine themselves in Our Lady's place or company seeing what she saw, and feeling the joy, sorrow and triumph that she experienced, it is most effectively communicating the fruits of its own contemplation to others. With the utmost simplicity it is using the words of an angel and of our Lord Himself, and the example of Our Lady, to lead its own members and a great band of the faithful to the contemplation of divine Truth; and that through all the processes of bodily movement, speech, imitative and constructive imagination, and reasoned consideration of the data of revelation which are set out by St. Thomas as the natural stages by which a good teacher must lead men to the Truth.

PRINTED IN GREAT BRITAIN BY
THE STANHOPE PRESS LTD
ROCHESTER : : KENT